(His)Story of Women:

The 'Second' Sex?

KACEY KELLS

———

(His)Story of Women:

The 'Second' Sex?

We cannot all succeed when half of us are held back".

Malala Yousafzai

Special thanks to Tom Gilroy who edited this book and to Francine for her unwavering support

TABLE OF CONTENTS

PROLOGUE

Do we really know who we are? Do we understand - not 'accept'!-our fate as women, why and how is it that we were -and still are- living in a man's world, dominated and often abused by our male counterparts? Is there any logic -not necessarily an 'acceptable' nor an irremediable logic- behind the fact that women and girls are often excluded from certain social, political and economic activities, when they are not simply excluded from public life? Does the almost universally admitted belief that women are the weaker sex constitute a scientifically admitted fact? Why is it that almost every society is ruled by men? And what are the consequences, not only for women and girls, but for modern societies and the challenges within that they must contend with?

Being a woman or a girl, a human female, is not an easy task! Our paths are full of interdictions, frustrations, humiliations of all sorts... just because we are females. Even when the law says that both genders have equal right, women face harder economic and social constraints: on average, wages are lower, employment opportunities are limited compared to men's and their participation in government affairs and politics remains generally low. Believe it or not: they are sometimes denied the right to control their bodies! When they try to stand up to defend their rights and the rights of their daughters, they are often ignored, mocked, or despised. Even if they can work and actively participate in the economic and social development of society, they are still seen and treated like second class citizens.

Since the domination of man over woman is a reality in almost every society, and because this sad and terrifying reality goes back to time immemorial, it is a fact generally accepted as some sort of intangible truth. Even in the most advanced societies, where gender equality is proclaimed, women and girls are still victims of minor and not-so-minor discrimination. Their inferiority to men is more or less universally admitted, even today, and even if we pretend otherwise. Hence, the question: are we really inferior to men? Because, if not, there is no reason to submit to them!... As we will see in the following pages, there is in fact no scientific reason to pretend that women and girls are inferior to men and boys; quite the contrary! The domination of women by men is not innate; it is not determined by the laws of nature! It's only a consequence of human history, a social and cultural phenomenon which is certainly not irreversible.

The domination of men over women is not only a despicable social phenomenon! Its consequences are severe, numerous, and dreadful. Way too often, women and girls suffer violence and sexual abuse. Domestic violence, sexual touching, and rape are commonplace and are often treated like petty crimes; but they are not! Those who abuse women or girls, humiliating them, are participants of a rape culture, the purpose of which is to crush women to dominate them and strengthen patriarchy. As a victim of rape, I learned this the hard way! I felt as if my life was shattered; I was overwhelmed with fear and shame, unable to speak, to explain what had really happened.

Instead of lodging a complaint with the police, I kept silent and tried to hide the truth; because, even if I was the victim and not the culprit, it was if I was trapped in bubble, unable to communicate and live a normal life... Fortunately, with the support provided by my mom and my counselor I finally found a way to break this bubble in which I had locked myself: I wrote, to describe what had happened to me in a memoir (*Kacey Kells, "Kellcey"*). That was a therapy. I have been lucky, but I know that it is not the case for everybody! I learned that women and girls are way too often victims of injustice. Hence, I decided to fight Rape Culture and Patriarchy, and to do so I had to start with demonstrating that the domination of women by men is not only unfair but scientifically groundless and, because it means the total or partial exclusion of fifty percent of the population, it is first and foremost extremely dangerous for the future of human societies.

(His)Story of Women: the 'Second' Sex?

Throughout history, and almost everywhere, from the earliest civilizations until today, women and girls have been treated as inferior beings, subjected to males' desires and violence. Trapped in a social, cultural and economic subordination, deprived of their fundamental rights, abused by tyrants who denied their humanity, they have been somehow condemned to suffer eternal hardships and unrelenting frustrations.

Consigned to a social, physical and intellectual 'inferiority' imposed by society at the beginning of the Neolithic Revolution, women were condemned to obedience, deprived of the right to express themselves in the public sphere, alienated and victimized. Therefore, they were soon described as impure creatures supposedly responsible for the sin and the misfortune that often strikes Mankind, hence justifying their social marginalization and the control and oppression of men over them.

*

Subjugating women and girls came to be an absolute priority which had to be achieved by all means possible, starting with the sanctification of women's 'flaws' and 'weaknesses'. It is not without reason that the Holy Book, the Ancient Testament, begins with a demons-tration and condemnation of the so called 'sins' of the 'weaker sex'! To show the inherent female 'inferiority', Genesis starts by saying that Eve, the first woman, was created after Adam by taking her from the rib of the latter who, unlike Eve, was made in the image of God! Moreover, Eve, who didn't eat the forbidden fruit, was made responsible for the 'crime', accused of being a temptress and the origin of the 'sin' -committed by Adam, who ate the apple! Therefore, if both were banished from Paradise, Eve's punishment was more severe than Adam's:

"To the woman God said: 'I will greatly multiply your pain in childbearing; in pain you shall bring forth children, yet your desire shall be for your husband, and he shall rule over you'" (*Genesis, 3:16; 4:1-2*).

Worse still, the punishment applied not only to Eve, but also to each and every one of her female descendants! It is not Eve who was chastised, but every woman and girl since... for ever and ever!!

*

Sadly, however, the Abrahamic religions are not the only misogynistic religions or ideologies! Even the Greco-Roman Pantheon, in spite of the existence of many goddesses along with the male gods, portrayed a rather misogynistic vision of the divine and human societies. After the original chaos came Gaia the first goddess and personification of Earth; she soon married Uranus, her son and personification of the sky. But because he was cruel with their common offspring, Gaia encouraged her son Cronos to emasculate her husband. Later, she supported the conspiracy of her daughter, Rhea, to overthrow Cronos; hence, with the support of his mother and grandmother, Zeus -Jupiter- came to power. And soon after, learning the lessons from his father and grandfather, he considered that the goddesses were a source of threat and instability and established a 'patriarchal government' to end the conspiracies supported by these females and the resulting turmoil.

It is also interesting to note the Olympian goddesses' characteristics. Three of them were virgins: Athena -Minerva-, who was represented and armed with male attributes -a sword, a helmet, a spear, and a shield. Artemis -Diana-, goddess of wilderness and chastity whose relationship with men was characterized by the myth of Actaeon -the young hunter who, because he saw her bathing naked was transformed into a deer by the angered goddess and devoured by his own hunting dogs; and Hestia -Vesta-, who swore to remain a maiden forever when the gods Apollo and Poseidon proposed to her. Needless to say they were not the typical representation of what one might consider as 'fully realized women'. As for the two other goddesses, Aphrodite -Venus-, they incarnated the supposedly inherent whimsical nature of women, and pure sexual love, while Hera -Juno-, Zeus's wife and goddess of marriage was always fighting with her husband!

"The goddesses are archetypal images of human females as envisioned by males. The distribution of desirable characteristics among a number of females rather than their concentration in one being is appropriate to a patriarchal society. The dictum of Pseudo-Demosthenes in the fourth century BC expresses the ideal among mortals: 'we have mistresses for our enjoyment, concubines to serve our person, and wives for the bearing of legitimate offspring'". [-] "A FULLY REALIZED FEMALE TENDS TO ENGENDER ANXIETY IN THE INSECURE MALE. Unable to cope with a multiplicity of powers united in one female, men from antiquity to the present have envisioned women in 'either-or' roles". (*Sarah B. Pomeroy, "Goddesses, whores, wives and slaves: women in Classical Antiquity"*).

*

The evolution of the Egyptian pantheon was also characterized by the seizure of goddesses' powers by male gods. In her thesis, Hilda Geissler explains:

"In the early dynastic era a powerful male dominated priesthood allied to the kings amalgamated and transformed pre-dynastic 'cults' of major goddesses in order to establish a state religion from the diverse local and regional cults. The position of king was endorsed by several goddesses with kings calling themselves their sons to substantiate their claims to power through their divinity. Spiritual emphasis shifted from renewal and regeneration through the goddess to male generation and self-renewal. Goddess power and roles were transmuted as creation/generation was acquired by the gods. The goddesses retained their transformation and regeneration functions for a time. As these roles became primary to religion, they were also acquired by the gods and goddesses became mere guides in roles where previously they had ruled" (*Hilda Geissler, "The role of the goddesses and the feminine in ancient Egyptian religion"*).

Here again, the transformation of society induced by the Neolithic Revolution led to a male dominated social environment and the spoliation of the goddesses' powers by their male counterparts.

Everywhere, the same process characterized Neolithic societies and, beside the empowerment of male gods at the expense of the existing goddesses, this contributed to the exclusive appropriation of power by men, and hence the strengthening of the domination of men over women and the establishment of patriarchy.

PART 1

THE MARGINALIZATION OF WOMEN

There is no certitude that human societies achieved gender equality before the Neolithic era (10,000 to 4,500 BCE), and even if some communities might have been ruled by females, this doesn't mean that these societies were matriarchal, as Sarah Pomeroy explains:

> "Of course, one woman who rules as a queen may enjoy the highest status, but her position does not empower her female subjects. As later well-documented historical periods show, a queen may

rule in a patriarchal society" (*Sarah B. Pomeroy, "Goddesses, whores, wives and slaves*).

There is one thing for sure, however: if the development of agriculture had a huge impact on human communities, it mostly had negative consequences for women and girls. Indeed, if the agricultural revolution led to the creation of settlements and the sedentary life of the Neolithic populations, it also contributed to exaggerate the gender division of labor and therefore induced a strengthened social and political structuration and stratification of the societies -hierarchy- where females became the weak link. With agriculture becoming the principal economic activity, there was a greater need for physical strength, hence relegating women and girls to the sideline. Skeletons excavated from the ancient city of Zheng Han, in China, show a severe aggravation of the dietary difference between genders during the Chinese Bronze Age (1700 to ~221 BC): males were better fed than females, and there was obviously more child malnutrition among girls than among their male counterparts (*Yu Dong, Chelsea Morgan...: "Shifting diets and the rise of male-biased inequality on the Central Plains of China during Eastern Zhou"*).

Gender discrimination, however, is not proper to China or to Asia. Tablets written in Linear B (earliest linear script in mainland Greece) found in Pylos, show that the food allotment for women in Greece was one third of the average male's ration during the Mycenaean Age (1100 – 600 BC) (*Sarah B. Pomeroy, "Goddesses, whores, wives and slaves, referring to F.F.J.Tritsh, "The Women of Pylos"*). Later, in Athens, an estimated 20% of female infanticides was 'institutionalized'; furthermore, in ancient Greece, women lifespan was at least 10 years less than men principally because of infanticides and neglect of female children (*Sarah B. Pomeroy, "Goddesses, whores, wives and slaves"*, referring to the works of Mark Golden and John Lawrence Angel). Obviously, female lives were not valued as much as male lives!!! And this is not typical to ancient societies: female infanticide remains a reality in today's world, particularly in China and in India among other countries; furthermore, in many regions of the world female children remain disadvantaged compared to boy children regarding their rights to education, life opportunities, and challenges.

Marginalization also means seclusion! In Greek city states, decent women had to stay in the gynæceum (women's quarters in the household) and, as we will see later, they were excluded from the public sphere: indeed, since public speaking was exclusively a male attribute, women had to remain silent and were not permitted to express themselves publicly; it was obviously inconceivable to let such weak and whimsical creatures rule the community or simply take any public responsibilities. And since the most important issues for pubescent and adult women were the risk of death in childbirth and the high level of child mortality -typical of every pre-industrial society-, women's lives were thus seen as being both fragile and essential (because of the need to give birth to many children to keep the population stable); hence, the 'justification' of their seclusion!

Actually, women's lives were mostly if not exclusively driven by their reproductive function:

"Pregnancy and childbirth must have dominated most women's lives" (*Mary Beard, "SPQR: a history of ancient Rome", 314*). "WOMEN ARE CREATURES WHO BLEED AND BREED" (*Sarah B. Pomeroy, "Goddesses, whores, wives and slaves"*).

This 'reproductive function', indeed, became their prison, the ultimate if not the only reason for their existence, their sole and unique 'raison d'être'. Put it simply, they were not seen as being fully human; rather, they were treated as mere objects, thus naturally and intrinsically inferior to men.

*

The idea, the belief that females, compared to the opposite sex, belong to a 'weaker' sex has always been the main pillar of any patriarchal society. And the exclusion of women from the public sphere… which led to their social, cultural, economic and political marginalization, and total subordination became the 'logical' and inescapable consequence of their status. To live and survive, women had no choice but to accept the absolute predominance and the tyrannical domination of men!

OBJECTIFICATION OF WOMEN

Excluded from the public sphere, unable to speak up and to express their ideas publicly, women were denied any right to engage in public life or public debate; and in return, they were forced to suffer the consequences of the decisions taken by men. Outside their household, they were treated like mere objects, dispossessed of human dignity; and even within their household, they were infantilized and forced to remain obedient and subservient to their male relatives.

> "One of the most compelling facts which can unite women and make us act is the overwhelming indignity or bitter hurt of being regarded as simply 'the other', 'an object', 'commodity', 'thing'" (*Sheila Rowbotham, Quotes, Goodreads*).

The title of Sheila Rowbotham's most famous book sums up the general idea: women were 'hidden from history'! (*Sheila Rowbotham, "Hidden from History"*). Dominated and silenced, it was as if women were absent from history; objects and not subjects, pale and insignificant shadows of their male counterparts, they were nothing! And they had no choice but to remain nothing because society, the economy, and politics belonged exclusively to males.

Women had to be and needed to be seen as being intrinsically weak to strengthen patriarchy; and to achieve their goal, men confiscated everything, every right that might have helped women to escape their prison. Hence, they opposed them owning and controlling even their own body, something that sadly still motivates the anti-abortion movements. Women were (and, still too often, are) prisoner of a body which is apparently not theirs.

So how could they control or decide about anything if they can't control and own their own body? Their objectification and their subordination to men therefore, appeared to be the inevitable and 'logical' consequence of their situation and inabilities. It was hence easy to doubt their intellectual capabilities and to stereotype them as inferior beings!

*

Consequently, women and girls were also deprived of relevant education; indeed, keeping females poorly educated or ignorant soon appeared to be one of the most efficient ways to secure the absolute domination of men. Hence, societies praised:

> "The weak elegancy of mind, exquisite sensibility and sweet docility of manners supposed to be the sexual characteristics of the weaker vessel!" (*Mary Wollstonecraft, "A Vindication of the Rights of Women"*). 'Be pretty and shut-up'!

Jean-Jacques Rousseau's famous assertion proves, among other things, that marginalizing women and girls remained an essential and powerful trait of societies throughout history until recent times, including Western society:

> "Men and women are made for each other, but their mutual dependence is not equal. ... We could survive without them better than they could without us. In order for them to have what they need ... we must give it to them, we must want to give it to them, we must consider them deserving of it. They are dependent on our feelings, on the

price we put on their merits, on the value we set on their attractions and on their virtues… Thus, women's entire education should be planned in relation to men. To please men, to be useful to them, to wins their love and respect, to raise them as children, care for them; as adults, counsel and console them, make their lives sweet and pleasant: these are women's duties in all ages and these are what they should be taught from childhood on." (Jean-Jacques Rousseau, "Emile").

Women were voluntarily kept in ignorance; they were silenced! And this soon became an imprescriptible rule in governing societies. Any transgression would have to be severely punished.

Throughout history, the education of women and girls was discouraged; learned women were generally seen as dangerous creatures, or evils. How many of them were abused, tortured, assassinated? Women had to remain inferior creatures and as such they were definitely not supposed to have access to education; they were not supposed to 'know', to teach, to discover or innovate. Only witches could do such things! And witches were burned at the stake!

*

Today, still, even if the literacy rate has significantly risen during the last decades and if, as a consequence, women are more educated worldwide than ever before, and if the gender gaps rarely persist in educated countries, two-thirds of the world illiterates are women (*Pamela Jakiela and Susannah Hares, "Mind the Gap: 5 Facts About The Gender Gap in Education", Center for Global Development + UNESCO Institute for Statistics, 2019*). When there is a situation of war, or civil war, girls are prevented from going to school more often than boys; in the poorest and most instable regions, when a family have two -or more- children, a boy and a girl, and if the cost of education is too high, they will chose to send their son(s) to school and keep their daughter(s) at home, because they certainly think that education is more important for a boy than for a girl!? It is probably why:

"If all developing regions have, or have almost achieved gender parity in primary education, the gender disparity widens at the secondary and tertiary school levels in many countries" (*UN Women, "Education", Sept. 20, 2021*).

And where there is no such problems, where the gender gap in education is low or nearly inexistent such as in Europe or in North America, women remain underrepresented in some sectors of employment or academic disciplines; it is particularly the case in Computer Science, and in the sectors of Information and Communication Sciences and Technology (*"Women in Informatics Research and Education", Informatics Europe*). Considering the very strategic importance of communication systems and informatics in modern society, it is no accident, and this is of course not without consequences for future generations. In the United States of America, women account for 47% of all employed adults, but hold only 24% of the technology positions (*Rebecca Koehn, Why Is There Still a Gender Gap in Tech?", Technopedia*). When asked to explain this situation, most women pointed out that they have experienced gender bias in their workplace. Communication sciences and

Technology are today seen as being strategic for the development of our society, and of course men have taken these sectors into their own control, turning the Tech culture into a macho culture.

THE FATE OF LEARNED WOMEN

Hypatia's horrible assassination in 415 testifies the brutality, viciousness and sadism that have infected men against learned women. Mathematician, astronomer, and philosopher, she was a leading intellectual of her time, the only woman for whom such claim can be made (*Britannica*). Admired by some, she nevertheless was the target of hatred by obscurantists.

"One day on the streets of Alexandria, Egypt, in the year 415 or 416, a mob of Christian zealots led by Peter the Lector accosted a woman's carriage and dragged her from it and into a church, where they stripped her and beat her to death with roofing tiles. They then tore her body apart and burned it". (*Sarah Zielinski, "Hypatia, Ancient Alexandria's Great Female Scholar", Smithsonian Magazine*).

Not only did they assassinate her, but they also humiliated her, stripping her naked publicly; then, they mutilated her before burning her dismembered body... Because killing a learned woman doesn't suffice!

*

Until recently Impersonal theoretical and scientific knowledge, the kind of knowledge privileged in the academy -and of course connected to 'Power'-, have been traditionally labelled in Western societies as being exclusively 'masculine', hence preventing women from acquiring and producing it. The argument to support the dogma was that giving access of this kind of knowledge to women would divert their vital energies from their 'natural' reproductive task (*Elizabeth Anderson, "Feminist epistemology: An interpretation and a defense", Hypathia, 1995*). Women were thereby almost exclusively confined to practical, untheoretical and undervalued knowledge acquired throughout their own life experience, such as the concerns of looking after children. This evil strategy proved to be extremely efficient in keeping women away from power and preserving -and strengthening!- patriarchy and androcentrism.

Over the centuries and millenniums, female scientists have made significant discoveries; but they were almost systematically attributed to their male colleagues or relatives; their names were written out of textbooks, their existence as scientists, denied. Back in ancient Greece, several women worked along with Pythagoras to understand the very nature of the universe; but this was a unique experience! And the real contribution of these few women has always been ignored since their works were published under Pythagoras's name (Éloïse Trouche, *"La place des femmes dans la recherche scientifique"*). Furthermore, after Pythagoras's death his documents were destroyed, not to mention the catastrophic loss of sources that had happened a few century later during the early Christian era. Our only certitude today is that 2,500 years ago, a group of men and women gathered together in Croton, in Southern Italy, united by the proposition that the universe is made of numbers and their love of intellectual exchange. Only one of these women mathematicians is known today: her name was Theano. But her real contribution is totally ignored and she is only remembered because she has been called the wife of Pythagoras! (*Dale Debakcsy,*

"Theano of Croton And The Pythagorean Women Of Ancient Greece).

During the Middle-Ages, until the XVIIIth century, women were strictly forbidden to have access to education and were consequently unable to contribute to science and technological development; any contributions would have been a crime condemned by the holy Church and most severely punished! By the XVIIIth century, however, some women -few- like Emilie du Chatelet worked in the development of science. But even during the XIXth and early XXth century, they were not considered as being capable of understanding scientific work and were only 'per-mitted' to work as 'volunteer' faculty, a subordinate status which kept them under control and at the mercy of men.

Later, during the XXth century, many brilliant academic women were frustrated, harassed, and defrauded! Lise Meitner's work in nuclear physics led to the discovery of nuclear fission in 1938, but she was excluded from the Nobel Prize which was attributed, in 1945, to her male colleagues: Otto Hahn and Fritz Strassmann (*Ruth Lewin Sime, "Lise Meitner, a life in Physics"*). Thanks to her work on the X-ray diffraction images, Rosalind Franklin discovered the helix structure of DNA in 1951, but the Nobel Prize was given to Jim Watson, Francis Crick and Maurice Watkins who plundered her work and published 'their' discovery without mentioning Rosalind Franklin's name (*Matthew Cobb, "Sexism in science: did Watson and Crick really steal Rosalind Franklin's data?"*). Jocelyn Bell Burnell was another wronged heroine: in 1967, she discovered Pulsars, a remnant of massive stars that went supernova; but she was still a graduate student and was excluded from the Nobel Prize which was given to Antony Hewish, her supervisor, and Martin Ryle. Esther Lederberg, discovered a virus that affects bacteria (lambda bacteriophage) in 1951, but the Nobel Prize was given to her husband, Joshua Lederberg, who later admitted that 'she deserved credit' for that discovery (*Jane Lee, "6 Women Scientists Who Were Snubbed Due to Sexism"*). In 1905, Nettie Stevens discovered sex chromosomes and identified the role of chromosomes X and Y in sex determination; but she died of breast cancer and a few years later the Nobel Prize of Medicine was given to Thomas Hunt Morgan, her thesis director (*Kaitlin Smith, "Nettie Maria Stevens - 1861-1912"*)

The list of academic women who were or still are victim of abuse and spoliation is endless. Even today, gender discrimination in sciences often remains a reality: Tim Hunt, 2001 Nobel Prize of Medicine, said to the World Conference of Science Journalists in Seoul, in 2015, that scientists should work in gender-segregated labs because "'girls' cause men to fall in love with them and cry when criticised"!!! (*Rebecca Ratcliffe, "Nobel scientist Tim Hunt: female scientists cause trouble for men in labs"*). According to UNESCO, female researchers account for only 29.3% of total researchers around the world (*"Women in Science"*, *UNESCO Institute of Statistics*). However, this figure conceals huge disparities between the different regions of the world with a total of 32.7% female researchers for North America and Western Europe - only!-, and 48.2% for Central Asia and 18.5% for South and West Asia. Surprisingly, the so-called Western World is not the best place to be for women scientists!

*

Power is

> "The ability to control people and events" (*Cambridge Dictionary*); it is "the capacity to direct or influence the behavior of others or the course of events" (*Oxford Language*).

Power is the exercise of authority; it presupposes expertise and knowledge! Thus, denying women the same right to education and knowledge than men is denying them access to power. Hence, the exclusive and entire appropriation of power by males at the expense of females, who consequently become their property. In such a context, potentially powerful women are often seen as being extremely dangerous creatures who could destabilize the society -and men's domination-, and who consequently should be eliminated in any way possible.

SILENCING WOMEN

Women must be silenced! This is an absolute necessity to secure a healthy patriarchy! Even today, in our so-called 'modern' society, if women work with men and participate in meetings... and even if they generally are not formerly silenced, it is still more complicated for a woman to express herself publicly in a society dominated by men. There are numerous strategies and means to silence women and girls. Mockery and harassment are some of them! The idea is to humiliate or intimidate the victims in order to shush them up. Bullying and intimidation are still very common practices within boardrooms, especially when men outnumber their female counterparts. And what about cyber bullying? Virginija Langbakk, Director of the European Institute for Gender Equality -EIGE- sums up the situation as follows:

"Digital spaces can be empowering places of opinion-formation, debate and mobilisation. However, cyberbullying restricts the opportunities offered by digitalisation. Young people, especially women are put off from taking part in political discussions or online debates. All of society is missing out when young women are not engaged because we are losing their potential to get involved in politics and become future leaders," ("*Cyberbullying restricts young women's voices online*").

Females are more likely than males to suffer from online harassment; according to the European Institute for Gender Equality, 9% of young women declare being victim of online hate-speeches and online abuse compared to 6% of young men. As Mary Beards points out, it is not what the women say that matters; it is the fact that they express themselves publicly; they simply shouldn't! If they are permitted to show something publicly, it is their naked body! Following this logic, their intimacy is sometimes stolen and aired in public against their will… because these men consider that females are only mere objects without rights or pride; because they see them as their 'property' they share the certitude that women should be denied any access to the public sphere… should be denied the right to express their ideas by all available means! As mentioned above, only the anatomy of these 'inferior beings' can be shown publicly: a 'pleasant' way, indeed, to silence the 'weaker sex'! Therefore, the contribution of pornography to Patriarchy: it helps depreciate women's image and status.

Silencing women necessarily involves the use of violence and threat! Violence can, of course, take different forms: mockery, shouting, sexual fondling… rape. Violence against women can be everywhere: at home, in the subway, at the workplace, online. Hence the sense of insecurity shared by every girl and every woman, a sense of insecurity that often cripples them! Abusing women is embedded in male culture, and since our societies have long been male-dominated systems… there is no choice but to change the society to make it compatible with both genders.

During the last few decades, our society has changed, fortunately. Women's rights are sometimes enshrined in law, or in the constitution. Nowadays, in most countries, abusing a woman in public is not 'politically' correct, and might even constitute a criminal offence!

But it would be extremely naïve to believe that women are not victimized anymore, even in its worst forms: Harvey Weinstein's scandal, which was the origin of the MeToo movement, President Trump's gendered language and behavior -at best!-, the impoverishment of women due to pandemics or other crisis, the comeback of the Talibans and their segregationist gender policies, Boko Haram which has systematically abused girls and women in Nigeria and the rise in feminicide worldwide during and after the Covid-19 pandemics (*"UN Women raises awareness of the shadow pandemic of violence against women during COVID-19"*)… not to mention the situation of women and girls in Saudi Arabia and in many other countries! These terrifying facts and events testify that gender segregation, sexual abuse and oppression are definitely not behind us.

*

However, there are historically two contextual exceptions where women have been permitted to speak publicly: when they are speaking as victims or martyrs, to denounce the crimes they have suffered; or when they speak to defend their home, children, husbands, or in the interests of OTHER WOMEN. In other words, under certain specific occasions, they might be permitted to defend their 'sectional interests', but never to speak for men or for the whole community (*Mary Beard, "Women and Power"*).

One of the very first examples came when Rome refused to abolish the discriminatory Oppian Law. After its disastrous defeat at the hands of Hannibal at the battle of Cannae in 216 BC, Rome, whose economy was in shambles, passed the Oppian Law supposedly to restrict 'female extravagance' and tap into women's wealth, and hence restore its budget. The law went so far as to rule that women's tunics should not be of different colors and forbid them from riding in carriages! Driven by patriotic feelings, Roman matrons initially obeyed the new law and gave their gold willingly (*The Luxury and the Lex Oppia, Rome and Art*); but a few years later, in 195 BC, when some tribunes refused to repeal the discriminatory law despite the improvement of the general economic situation, women -who had no political power!-

poured into the Forum and blocked the streets and the houses of the tribunes who wanted to maintain the Oppian Law! It was the first time such an event led by women was seen in Rome (*"Lex Oppia", Oxford Research Encyclopedia*), and it incurred the wrath of the conservative tribunes as attested by Cato's speech:

'Citizens of Rome, if each one of us had set himself to retain the rights and the dignity of a husband over his own wife, we should have less trouble with women as a whole sex. As things are, our liberty, overthrown in the home by female indiscipline, is now being crushed and trodden underfoot here too, in the Forum. It is because we have not kept them under control individually that we are now terrorized by them collectively. I really used to think it a fable, a piece of fiction - that story of the destruction, root and branch, of all the men on that island by a conspiracy of the women" (*Cato the Elder is speaking, 195 BCE, on the repeal of the Lex Oppia, "Livy 34.4-7"*).

But the women's demonstrations intensified, and Cato and his supporters were forced not use their veto. For the first time, women imposed their will!

A few years later, in 42 BC, while Rome was being ravaged by the civil war after Julius Caesar's assassination, the ruling Triumvirs Octavian, Antony, and Lepidus were unable to raise enough money, so they decided to tax the 1,400 wealthiest women in Rome. The latter, fearing that these taxes could be used in battles against their own families, protested and asked Hortensia, the educated daughter of Quintus Hortensius, a renowned orator, to speak for them:

> "You have already stolen from us our fathers and sons and husbands and brothers by your proscriptions, on the grounds that they had wronged you. But if you also steal from us our property, you will set us into a state unworthy of our family and manners and our female gender. If you claim that you have in any way been wronged by us, as you were by our husbands, proscribe us as you did them. But if we women have not voted

any of you public enemies, if we did not demolish your houses or destroy your army or lead another army against you; if we have not kept you from public office or honour, why should we share the penalties if we have no part in the wrongdoing? Why should we pay taxes when we have no part in public office or honours or commands or government in general, an evil you have fought over with such disastrous results?" (*I.M. Plant, "Women Writers of Ancient Greece and Rome": Hortensia's Speech Rome, 42 B.C.*).

The triumvirs were of course upset and tried to drive the women away, but the crowds in the Forum Romanum supported the women and so the triumvirs conceded to reduce the number of women required to pay the tax from 1400 to 400 and instituted a tax on all men of a certain level of wealth. That was a second -and ultimate- women's victory. However, to paraphrase Mary Beard, they only defended their 'sectional interest'.

*

Sadly, such victories are seldom in human history! Silencing women was the rule in ancient Greece, in Rome, during the Middle Ages, Renaissance and after; not only in Europe but almost everywhere! And today, the rule remains, more aggressively in some places like Afghanistan or Saudi Arabia than elsewhere… but it remains! As pointed out by Mary Beard, still the most important speeches made by women, like Hilary Clinton's famous speech at the United Nations General Assembly in 1995, concern women and women's rights… and when exceptionally a woman speaks up publicly for other purposes, she is seen and described as having an androgynous mind or something.

Yes, the situation has changed, especially during the last decades and the last century; throughout the world, there are more women who express themselves and who participate in society! The United Nations Organisation with UN-Women, created in 2010, promotes women's rights and women empowerment through a series of initiatives. More importantly, UN-Women, along with several feminist associations, is working to change the minds and stereotypes we have of women, fighting against discrimination that affect women and girls. But there is still a long way to go!

Even if there are more women in executive government positions and in national parliament worldwide than ever before, they are still underrepresented and the resistance to their ascension remains high, and sometimes violent as shown during the 2016 Presidential campaign in the United States where Hilary Clinton was regularly, violently aggressed and threatened (*J.Y Watson, "There Will Be Blood: At a Donald Trump rally, supporters call for the death of Hillary Clinton"; "Witch Hunt Rhetoric Against Hillary Clinton Will Stain The GOP Forever"*), going so far as threatening to put her head on a spike! (*"Witch Hunt Rhetoric At Trump Rallies Continues To Repel Women"*).

"Across the world, an alarming 40 percent of women Members of Parliament surveyed in 39 countries have received threats of kidnap, assault, rape, death, or the abduction of their children while in office. One-fifth of MPs reported being subjected to sexual violence" (*Marie Berry, "Violence against women in politics"*).

Violence against female politicians is systemic in many developing countries; in her above-mentioned article, Marie Berry relates how a group of Kenyan women politicians she met recently explained:

"Their biggest fear in running for office was being physically attacked or stripped naked in the street" (*M. Berry, "Violence against women in politics"*).

However, violence against female politicians is not unique to developing countries. The above-mentioned ignominious attacks against Hillary Clinton, or the killing in the United Kingdom of MP Helen Joanne Cox who was shot and stabbed to death in 2016 prove it.

*

In any case, if the participation of women as members of the executive and/or the legislative is a necessity to improve governance everywhere, it won't suffice to promote gender equality and empower women and girls! Let's quote Sarah B. Pomeroy again:

"One woman who rules as a queen may enjoy the highest status, but her position does not empower her female subjects"!

We need more and better changes, in every society, to eradicate all kind of gender discrimination, from birth to death. We need a global cultural change!

FEMINISM AND WOMEN'S RIGHTS

Throughout history, several brilliant women, like Mary Wollstonecraft (1759-1797), called for gender equality. Of course, given the overwhelming influence of the Church and the overwhelming cultural obscurantism that reigned all over Europe during the Middle Age, it was as if women were metaphorically asphyxiated, unable to express any idea. Fortunately, things changed slightly during the late Middle-Age and Renaissance: in the late XIVth and early XVth centuries, Christine de Pisan wrote several books, discussing many feminist topics, including the source of women's oppression and misogyny, the need of education for women, women's rights and the vision of a more equal world. In "Le Dit de la Rose" (*"The Tale of the Rose"*), she opposed the misogynistic idea that women only came to this world to seduce men, and in her two greatest works -"La Cité des Dames" (*"The City of the Ladies"*) and "Le Trésor de la Cité des Dames" (*"The Treasure of the City of Ladies"*)- she discussed the oppression of women and defended their capabilities and virtues. Christine de Pisan's aim was to provide a powerful positive image of women - warriors, scientists, artists...- to help future generations fight misogyny:

> "Not all men -and especially the wisest- share the opinion that it is bad for women to be educated. But it is very true that many foolish men have claimed this because it displeased them that women knew more than they did." (*Christine de Pisan, "The book of the city of Ladies"*).

I will not here enumerate every woman who has tried to contribute to promote women's rights from the Late Middle-Age until today. In any case, they had something in common: their task wasn't easy, as Olympe de Gouges' personal story shows. This French woman published 'The Declaration of the Rights of Women and Female Citizens', during the French Revolution in 1791. She was simply asserting that women had intrinsically the same rights as men! But the male revolutionists and the Terror that reigned as a consequence of Robespierre's policy sadly followed

Jean-Jacques Rousseau's 'philosophical' guidelines and were not ready to give females the rights they claimed for themselves. Hence, Olympe de Gouges was sentenced to death and beheaded! ... because she dared ask for equality among genders!

*

The first feminist movement, or collective initiative, came in July 1848 with the Seneca Falls Convention - NY-, where Elizabeth Cady Stanton declared:

"We are assembled to protest against a form of government, existing without the consent of the governed—to declare our right to be free as man is free, to be represented in the government which we are taxed to support, to have such disgraceful laws as give man the power to chastise and imprison his wife, to take the wages which she earns, the property which she inherits, and, in case of separation, the children of her love". (*"Seneca Falls Convention", History.com*).

It is not surprising that the main demand of the early feminist movements concerned the right to vote -the 'sacred right to the elective franchise'. That was the very first step to fight exclusion and marginalization: to give a voice to women! But even that wasn't an easy task, and women sometimes had to engage in direct actions and civil disobedience, like the Suffragettes in the United Kingdom led by Emmeline Pankhurst in the early XXth century. In 1893 New Zealand became the first sovereign state to accept giving women the right to vote; then, came Australia in 1902, and Finland in 1906. The United Kingdom granted suffrage to women over 30 -only!- in 1918. The United States of America ratified the 19th amendment -which granted women the right to vote- in 1920; and in France, women had to wait until 1945, one century after the introduction of the universal suffrage -for men!. In Saudi Arabia, they had to wait until 2015.

But the right to vote does not suffice to promote gender equality and to prevent the marginalization of women! Emma Goldman, a radical feminist, explained in the early XXth century that the ballot didn't secure equality among men and women and hence wouldn't help to secure gender equality. The only way women could gain freedom was:

> "by refusing the right to anyone over her body; by refusing to bear children, unless she wants them; by refusing to be a servant to God, the State, society, the husband, the family, etc., by making her life simpler, but deeper and richer" (*Emma Goldman, "Anarchism and Other Essays*).

With the massive entry of women in the workplace during the XXth century, their socio-economic situation and participation in society changed dramatically, asking mechanically for more liberty, equality of rights, and opportunities for women. The acquisition of the right to vote by women was now clearly insufficient to lessen social, economic and political inequalities among genders. Women and girls were still treated like second class citizens, suffering all sorts of discrimination. Thus, the 'Second wave of Feminism' fought to achieve equal civil rights in the late 1960s and 1970s. The principal demands were to end employment discrimination, unequal pay, and legal inequality. Apart from these objectives, the

Second wave of Feminism was also concerned with other issues, including sexuality and family. Domestic violence, marital rape, or simply the overwhelming male dominance over females in the family became key aspects of the fight for the rights of women and against gender discrimination. In fact, these claims corresponded to the evolution of Western Society: since women were better educated and became financially more independent, they naturally claimed for greater progress in the area of civil rights.

*

The above-mentioned examples show that Feminism is not a strict or rigid doctrine but evolves with society and its cyclical situation. It's a process which aims to ultimately reach one objective: the end of gender discrimination.

ABORTION RIGHTS

With the second wave, women also started to fight for reproductive rights (legal rights and freedoms relating to reproduction and reproductive health), including abortion rights. Indeed, women's role changed from being mostly seen as child bearer to economic actor. They were progressively given easier access to education. In other words, their socio-economic status improved. In consequence, controlling fertility not only became a possible issue -thanks to the progress of science and contraception- but something acceptable and even desirable. Indeed, reducing the birth rate was the logical consequence of the greater participation of women in the labor force. Regarding abortion rights, however, things were -and often remain- more complicated, and decriminalizing abortion is still a difficult and challenging task for women and girls in many countries.

"At the end of the twentieth century, abortion was legally permitted to save the life of the woman in 98% of the world's countries.13 The proportion of countries allowing abortion on other grounds was as follows: to preserve the woman's physical health (63%); to preserve the woman's mental health (62%); in case of rape, sexual abuse, or incest (43%); fetal anomaly or impairment (39%); economic or social reasons (33%); and on request (27%)" (*Marge Berer, "Abortion Law and Policy Around the World"*).

*

Why is it that legal abortion constitutes an imperative social, health, and ethical issue? Let's discuss health reasons first: abortion is one of the safest medical procedures if done following the World Health Organization's -WHO- guidance; however, it is the cause of at least one in six maternal deaths from complications when it is performed secretly, without safe procedure (*Marge Berer, "Abortion Law and Policy Around the World"*...). Furthermore, since unintended pregnancy is associated with an increased risk of problems for the mom and her baby, it should be seen as a key social issue, profitable to the society.

It is also, undeniably, an important question of ethics; because, allowing woman the right to make choices about when they want to have children in relation to their age, financial stability & relationship stability, is or should be considered as a natural right; it is a fundamental right! Certainly, it is not the role and the mission of a democratic government to legislate against women's choices.

Thanks to better access to contraceptive services, the situation of course has improved and the proportion of unintended pregnancies has severely fallen during the last decades. Nevertheless, many women still experience at least one unintended pregnancy before the age of 45 years, especially in the poorest regions. Worse, as a result of the fast expansion of the world population, the percentage of unintended pregnancies ending in abortion has increased! And this is even more true in countries where abortion rights are restricted (*"New Estimates Show Worldwide Decrease in Unintended Pregnancies"*, *Guttmacher Institute, July 23, 2020*).

"The proportion of unintended pregnancies ending in abortion was 51% in 1990–1994, and it stayed roughly the same through 2000–2004. It then increased to 61% by 2015–2019" *("Unintended Pregnancy and Abortion World-wide", Guttmacher Institute, Fact Sheet, July 2020)*.

*

Beyond these facts, it seems normal to assert that every society, everywhere, should view women and girls as full human beings. And human beings are supposed to be responsible beings! In consequence, women should be seen and treated like responsible beings, such as their male counterparts. Therefore, why shouldn't they be given full sovereignty over their own body? There is certainly no need for a government to act as a surrogate of its citizens. No ideology, no religion, no institution should be permitted to have a hold on women and girls, or to diminish their rights!

RAPE CULTURE AND GENDER BASED VIOLENCE

Patriarchy and the objectification of women and girls have stiff consequences for our societies, and the worst is certainly Rape Culture. Based on a dichotomy opposing 'manhood', seen as intrinsically dominant and sexually aggressive, and 'womanhood', whose main characteristics are to be submissive and sexually passive, Rape Culture is the ultimate weapon to subjugate and humiliate the 'weaker'sex. Indeed, such a perspective tends to justify the perpetuation of sexual violence and abuse because it implicitly postulates that females should be sexually dominated by males! This is the final step in the objectification of women and girls!... and, sadly, it is still deeply enshrined in our male-dominated cultures.

"Rape Culture is an environment in which rape is prevalent and in which sexual violence against women is normalized and excused in the media and popular culture. Rape culture is perpetuated through the use of misogynistic language, the objectification of women's bodies, and the glamorization of sexual violence, thereby creating a society that disregards women's rights and safety" (*"Rape Culture", Women's and Gender Center*).

As shown in the quote above, Rape Culture is multifaceted and complex. It starts with apparently insignificant trivial comments, it is not visible at first; it is conveyed and propagated by the way we educate children, the stereotypical view of boys and girls by their family and society. Indeed, studies show that, from the most conservative to the most liberal countries, children at an early age internalize this myth that girls are vulnerable and dependent -their body and beauty being their main preoccupation- while boys are supposed to be strong and independent.

"It has long been suggested that during adolescence, the world expands for boys and shrinks for girls, but the new study, which looked at kids in Bolivia, Belgium, Burkina Faso, China, the Democratic Republic of Congo, Ecuador,

Egypt, India, Kenya, Malawi, Nigeria, Scotland, South Africa and the U.S., emphasizes how global that phenomenon is and how young it sets in" (*Belinda Luscombe, "Kids Believe Gender Stereotypes by Age 10, Global Study Finds"*).

We understand then why fighting gender stereotypes is both a critical and extremely complex issue. Complex, because it is deeply rooted in the fundamentals of our societies, and critical because it is the only way to end gender inequality and violence against girls and women. However, in spite of the frequent calls for the elimination of domestic violence and sexual violence against women, an estimated 736 million women and girls aged 15 years old or older have experienced physical or sexual violence by a partner, or sexual violence by a non-partner, at least once in their lifetime (*"Progress on the Sustainable Development Goals: the Gender Snapshot", UN Women*).

*

Rape Culture has huge repercussions, both on individuals and on the society. Victims of sexual assault not only suffer an ignominious crime, but they also suffer the consequences! A rape is not just a terrifying physical aggression: its effects on victims are immeasurable: they are mentally destroyed, they feel defiled, humiliated, weak, useless... Shame and terror are paralyzing agents and might drive them insane and totally unable to grow.

> "Survivors have to... 'we' have to live with this for the rest of our lives, long after the crime was committed. It is as if we'd been branded, burnt with hot iron. Therefore, assaulting, raping someone, anyone, whatever her age, is anything but an ordinary crime because the abuser(s) not only break their victim on the day they rape her, but they also instil poison in her soul; and this will unavoidably devastate her existence" (*Kacey Kells, "Kellcey"*).

There are ways to heal, of course... but the stigma will remain anyway: panic attacks, nightmares, solitude, difficulty to communicate face to face, overwhelming feeling of exhaustion because -you can't help yourself!- you are permanently on your guard... Under such circumstances, it is extremely hard for the victims to grow and help the society grow. They are tempted to stay on the sidelines, self-marginalized, ashamed of a crime they didn't commit, scared to death for the rest of their lives… trapped in their solitude! And this is certainly the same for many victims of domestic violence.

Rape Culture, however, doesn't only affect the unfortunate victims who have been assaulted. Every girl and every woman, even the most privileged among them, keep this somewhere in her head: 'this could happen to me!'; 'I could be the victim of a sexual aggression!'. The fear is everywhere: in the streets, in the subway, in the workplace, when we go jogging… even at home and when we are online. For a woman, threats are everywhere, anytime! Of course, this is not without consequences… for our psychological wellbeing and for the community. Abuse against women and girls take different forms: forced marriage, social and economic restrictions, genital mutilations.

Over 200 million women and girls in 31 countries have undergone female genital mutilation. In half of the countries with available data, the majority were cut before the age of 5 (*"Progress on the Sustainable Development Goals: The gender snapshot 2021"*, UN Women). Moreover, UN Women estimates that in some countries over 50% of girls from poor rural household will be married as children (*"Learn the facts: Rural women and girls"*, UN Women, October 2021*).

Yes, this is obvious: Rape Culture and violence against women and girls are the ultimate instruments of discrimination against women and girls! They permit the marginalization and subjugation of women and girls in every society, everywhere. Hence, far from being ordinary crimes, they constitute the most efficient instruments of men's power and patriarchy! Obviously, the reign of patriarchy is the reign of tyranny and fear!

PART 2

EMPOWERING WOMEN TO MEET THE CHALLENGES THREATENING THE FUTURE OF MANKIND

"A balanced and strong society cannot treat girls and women as a weak link; rather, it must see them as a full part of the community. A society cannot achieve all its potential if such discriminations remain" (*Kacey Kells, "Kellcey"*).

"The most basic and important premise for women's empowerment is peace and the absence of violence, including domestic violence" (*Lisa Warth, Malinka Koparanova, "Empowering Women for Sustainable Development", Discussion Papers Series 2012-1, United Nations Economic Commission for Europe*).

During the last decades, we have seen a slight proportional decline of the population of females in the world, principally because of the one child policy in China which caused a rise of female infanticides and also because of the high level of unborn girls illegally aborted in India (*"Population, female % of total population", World Bank; "India accounts for 45.8 million of world's missing females over last 50 years: UN report"*). However, with 49,58% of the total world population, the number of females is almost equal to the male population. But they are still victims of discrimination of all sorts, when they are not completely marginalized. The return of the Taliban to power in the summer of 2021, Boko Haram's abductions of child girls and forced marriages, the situation of women in Saudi Arabia... are among the best known examples of extreme abuse committed nowadays against girls and women... Unfortunately, the list of systematic abuse and crimes committed against women to marginalize them is endless!

Yet, we need every skill, every talent, and every brain to meet the critical challenges that threaten the future of mankind. Global warming, biodiversity losses and environmental degradation, famine as a result of unequal resource distribution, human overpopulation, pandemics fostered by ever-growing communications... There are all sorts of new global risks that might threaten our future!

If the comfort of modern life and the apparent safety provided by contemporary society gives an illusion of immutability and stability, the world, our world, is to a certain extent actually becoming more unsafe -and potentially unstable- than ever before! Thanks to the techno-scientific progress which is in constant acceleration, the dynamics of change is following at an even greater pace. Therefore, we need to be more flexible, more imaginative and efficient to address the challenges stemming from this fast acceleration of the pace of change and the extremely complex range of issues that we -will- have to face. We urgently need to do our best and put all the odds on our side. And to do so, we need everyone, regardless of their gender, racial, or religious differences.

We need everyone, and everyone's best skills; and this will only be possible if we give equal access to education and equal opportunities to women and girls. It is precisely the meaning of gender equality and women empowerment. The idea is not to take revenge, or to launch a gender war! Quite the contrary! We need to work together, to understand that we are all in the same boat, that each of us is capable, and that we need every skill and expertise.

Females add up to nearly fifty percent of the world population: hence, providing the same educational and employment opportunities to both genders will mathematically help increase innovation, and this will be an absolute necessity to meet the new challenges that will confront us. If there is no employment discrimination, women's average wage and power purchase will rise, thus boosting demand and production. And if we can secure equal educational and employment opportunities, we will become collectively more successful in every sector of activity and innovation. It is the only way to meet the challenges that will undoubtedly be posed by the rise of the above-mentioned global risks.

*

Marginalization means exclusion; hence, marginalizing nearly fifty percent of the population is complete nonsense! Especially today, when we urgently need improved skills and enhanced innovation. Hence, because it feeds a system that segregates females, we can now say that if patriarchy is a horrendous system inherited from the dark ages, it is also harmful and extremely dangerous for the future of modern societies. The chances of survival of Mankind, or at least the perpetuation of human civilization as we know it would be very slight without the inclusion of women and girls in every sphere of the society. Empowering women is not just a question of rights or ethics; it is the only way to ensure our collective survival!

THE CYCLE OF WOMEN'S POVERTY

Everywhere in this world, women are like the poor stepchildren of Mankind; they are more likely than men to live in poverty. There work is undervalued and their wages are systematically lower than men's. Globally, women earn 24% less than men (*"Why the majority of the world's poor are women?", OXFAM International*); and this is when they are given a wage! Often, especially in the poorest countries, women have little chance to get a real job, with a wage; therefore, they remain dependant on men. Yet, women work more than men! If the latter spend more time at work than women, the gender division of labor hides a harsh reality; there is a difference between 'being at work' and 'working': the difference between paid and unpaid work. And, everywhere, women perform the majority of unpaid domestic work.

Preparing and cooking meals, cleaning, washing clothes, collecting water and fuel, caring for children and sometimes older persons are the common tasks which are traditionally reserved for women. And even if they have paid work and stay the whole day at their workplace, they will spend the rest of the time in household work.

> "Women do at least twice as much unpaid care work, such as childcare and housework, as men – sometimes 10 times as much, often on top of their paid work. The value of this work each year is estimated at least $10.8 trillion – more than three times the size of the global tech industry" (*"Why the majority of the world's poor are women?", OXFAM International*)

According to the same sources, a young woman will work the equivalent of four years more than a man over her lifetime. Worse, way too often women have no choice but to bring up children on their own, either because they are single or because they have been abandoned by their husband. In any case, most of the time, when a parent decides to go away to live a better life, it is the female who stays with the children and has the responsibility to educate and to take care of them. Of course, such a situation is not without consequences: since single mothers care for their children –'their' should normally mean that both parents are responsible for their children!-, they have less time for other activities: work, education, hobbies...; they also have fewer financial and material resources... Thus, they are often trapped between poverty and marginalization! And such circumstances are generally the cause of individual, familial, and social tragedy. Because children, also, suffer the consequences of poverty: lack of education, poor sanitary conditions, feeling of insecurity that might lead to social maladjustment and delinquency.

Sadly, the general situation is not improving satis-fyingly. The United Nations Organisation estimates that 70% of the people in poverty worldwide are women; women and girls represent 60% of all undernourished people in the worl (*"Women and hunger Facts", Hunger Notes, www.worldhunger.org*). Consequently, these popu-lations are extremely vulnerable, especially when there is a crisis, and the consequences for their children are often dramatic. It is sadly a fact that women in poverty also suffer from a lack of human rights protection and from discrimination; UN Women states that 55% of women with newborn babies receive no maternity cash benefits.

Whenever there is a social crisis, females, because they are marginalized and in fragile situations compared to males, suffer more than the opposite sex; that was true back in ancient times, and is still true today. The Covid-19 pandemic had a disastrous impact on women and girls and reversed progress in expanding women's rights and opportunities. Of course, the most vulne-rable among them, including migrants, ethnic minority women, women and girls with disabilities, and those affected by conflict, are frequently 'left behind', and hence further marginalized. Between 2019 and 2021, 13.4 million women lost their jobs compared with 0.9% for men -in Europe, the loss for both genders was approximately the same. Women's food insecurity levels were 10% higher than men's in 2020, compared with 6% higher in 2019.

"Women have not recovered lost jobs and income, hunger is on the rise, and school closures threaten girls' educational gains" (*"Progress on the Sus-tainable Development Goals: The gender snapshot 2021", UN Women*).

*

Even when the situation is less severe, even in the privileged segment of our societies, the economic gender gap is blatant. Most of the time, women have lower wages than men for the same job; and we should not forget that they are often given precarious or lower quality jobs. Why is it so? The fact that women and girls do not have the same education than boys and men is a logical and valid explanation, of course; but it is fortunately less the case today in advanced economies where more and more females receive higher education. The causes are elsewhere! A few years ago, I was chatting with a group of male business students; when the discussion came up about the relevance for small or large companies of employing women, they all agreed that this was an unnecessary risk since women become pregnant and are consequently often missing…??? So what? Should we stay home… or should we stop having babies?

These people were 'educated' young men from one of our best universities… but they still think and behave as if girls and women were illiterate louts! Is it then surprising that in some universities female students are still subject to discrimination and sexual abuse?

Let's take some examples to illustrate the phenomenon of generalized -universalized- female poverty! If both husband and wife have a car, the modern and powerful one will most of the time belong to him, while she drives the older car. At bus stops, the proportion of adult females is often higher than the number of adult males, because the latter have more chances to own a vehicle… and if a couple own only one car or motorcycle, the privilege to drive it will almost systematically -quasi-exclusively- be given to the man. As mentioned above, women's median weekly earnings is everywhere inferior to men's median weekly earnings, even if the law stipulates equal pay for equal work: $900 for women, $1,089 for men in 2021 in the USA (*U.S. Bureau of Labor Statistics*); in France, women's pay is 24% inferior to men's (*"Les inégalités femmes-hommes en 12 chiffres et 6 graphiques", Le Monde, June 15, 2019*); and in the United Kingdom in 2020, men in their 40s earnt an average of 725 British pounds a week, while women earnt only 609 pounds a week (*"Median weekly earnings for full-time employees in the United Kingdom in 2020, by age and gender", Statista*).

Besides, in the case of divorce, women are more affected than men, and one in five women fall into poverty as a result. In the United States, about one in three women who own a home and have children at home when they divorce lose their homes. Three out of four mothers with child-support orders don't receive their full payment; consequently, they can't afford to keep their Health Insurance and must go through non-stop hell to support their family.

> "The financial burden is greatest during the first year after divorce and varies depending on: 1) how much money the woman contributed to the family income before divorce, and 2) the ability and willingness of her former husband to make child support payments (*"How Will Divorce Affect Me Financially? ", YourDivorceQuestions.Org*)

<u>BENEFITS AND PERKS OF DIVERSITY</u>

If it is obvious that we need every skill, every brain, every experience; if we understand that marginalizing or excluding whole segments of a community, in this case half of the population, is counter-productive and weakens our societies and their ability to address the current and emerging issues... the lot of women and girls must change, as soon as possible and everywhere to facilitate their total inclusion into the society and the economy! As previously stated, we cannot afford not to improve and sophisticate our technics and techno-logies, of course; we absolutely need to improve our knowledge and comprehension of this multifaceted world and the forces of change that drive it, so that we can adapt our strategies and answers, in ways to increase our collective efficiency.

Climate Change, the destruction of resources and biodiversity will undoubtedly pose new risks of unprecedented magnitude for the planet and for the species. And there is no planet B! We absolutely need to improve the governance of our societies, and this will not be possible if we do not include everyone. And we won't improve the governance if we do not include everyone! A society is a community, and it cannot grow satisfyingly if only a minority is concerned and feels responsible for the development of the whole commonwealth. It doesn't mean that we don't need elites! However, good governance requires that elites rule with the citizens, from the citizens and for the citizens... And here, we mean: for, from and with 'every' citizen! A stable and resilient society cannot exclude whole segments of the population, and the elite's shouldn't rule for the benefit of a few.

*

Since they were objectified and seen as nothing more than the property of their father, husband, son, family, or community, females were historically denied citizenship. But those long dark ages are fortunately over. Officially, at least, in most countries, females are today legally considered as equal to men, even if discrimination remains. As mentioned above, equality of rights presupposes equality of opportunities, equality of chances, and the absence of any kind of exclusion or marginalization -economic, cultural, educational, public security… But saying that everyone -males and females- are or should be equal does not mean that there are or should be no differences opposing the two genders. Certainly not!

The differences are obvious! They come from our physiological dissimilarities that separate the two sexes, and their psychological consequences. Because of their natural cycles, because they bear children, girls and women's lives and psyche are naturally unlike boys and men's lives and psyche. However, before going further in this analysis, I would like to warn the reader: some feminists will be reluctant to accept the idea of an existing intrinsic difference opposing the sexes, fearing that this might constitute an argument for further segregating females. I will try to demonstrate that they are wrong. Because we are intelligent people and we shouldn't hide or ignore the truth! We must in any circumstance proceed with objectivity and clear-sightedness!

Yes, females and males are physiologically and psychologically different; this doesn't mean that one gender is superior or inferior to the other! In fact, the differences opposing the sexes might even constitute an advantage for the community. In his analysis of the functioning of the international economy, Adam Smith insisted on the pact that the specialization of activities could be beneficial for every nation, because they could each produce what they are best at; and hence, thanks to the development of exchanges -trade-, sell their production at a good price and have access to other goods. In other words, economies benefit from their differences!

> "The division of labour, however, so far as it can be introduced, occasions, in every art, a proportionable increase of the productive powers of labour" (*Adam Smith, "The Wealth of Nations"*).

If Smith's theory has been somewhat nuanced by newer generations of economists, the general idea stipulating that the specialization of activities -division of labor- is positive for both parts and provides more efficiency and wealth is almost universally admitted. And there is no specialization without differences! I mean, it is because these nations are different that they can specialize their activities and become more efficient and wealthier. Actually, we could sum up this thinking saying that it is the existence of a diversity among nations which is the origin of growth and development. And this truth is not exclusively valid for economic activities.

If everybody-was educated in the same way, with the same knowledge, there would be no real possibility to learn from another. Here again it is our differences in terms of education, of culture, of expertise in scientific and artistic disciplines that make exchanges of knowledge, and consequently growth, possible.

If the existence of a diversity is seen as the greatest source of wealth, why would it be different when applied to the diversity that separates genders? The thing is, empowering women will bring much more than the simple addition or inclusion of a long marginalized population; since girls and women are equal but different, they can help the society grow thanks, not only to the addition of individual skills and expertise but, also, to the diversity they bring.

FEMALE PSYCHE

Culture, social norms, education, family and the community indubitably affect people's personality and contribute to the acquisition of gender stereotypes. From a very young age, little girls and little boys learn prescriptive social norms that call for gendered behavior and are encouraged to pursue gender-normative activities. Boys' color is blue and girls' is pink is the typical stereotype imposed by education and society. Girls wear skirts and boys trousers… but since the last few decades these stereotypes have been under attack, and everyone -supposedly- perfectly understands that women and girls can and do wear trousers too! Because we can all wear trousers… and since we are equal in right, we do so, if we wish to.

Still, we must note that if, today, women and girls are wearing trousers or skirts, it is most probable that boys and men won't agree to wear a skirt! Anyway, it is a fact that in modern societies, gender stereotypes, if they still exist, are less oppressive that they used to be. But if we agree that gender stereotypes strongly influence behavior and attitudes, does this mean that there is fundamentally no behavioral and psycho-logical difference opposing the two sexes? Does this mean that every such difference, every trait specific to men or to women is only the consequence of social learning and coercion, and that there is no gender behavior and psyche which is innate?... that there is intrinsically nothing typically male or typically female? Certainly not! This would be nonsense.

Females are made to carry their children in their womb. Their body is determined by their reproductive function and cycles. Their pelvis is larger than males, so that the baby they carry can safely leave their womb; their breasts are made to feed their newborns. Regularly their ovaries release eggs that could be fertilized by sperm... or not; if no pregnancy occurs, their uterus sheds its lining and they bleed, and in so doing they clean their womb for the next cycle and prepare their body for pregnancy. And because they carry and give life, they care.

Yes! Caring comes naturally to females; it is not just something they learned; it is not something imposed by society. It is in their genes, in their deepest nature. Back in time, women gave birth and cared for their children while men went hunting outside the cave; and because giving life and keeping their children alive could be tricky, they helped each other in case of need. Therefore, they inherited a strong sense of otherness. This is obvious when you look at group photos: if the persons on the photo are females, they will generally tilt their heads toward each other, but if this is a group of males, they usually don't. Actually, these gender traits are not exclusive to our species. Lionesses live in groups of females to care for their cubs while male lions are solitary animals; the same holds true for elephants and for a large variety of higher animals. And regarding species where both sexes are solitary, such as black bears, females care for their cubs and stay away from the males until the cubs are old enough to flee and live by themselves. There is indeed a wide variety of behavior in the animal world; but something is common to most species: females are more caring and tend to be more communal than males.

Humans obey the same rule: women have a greater sense of otherness than men who are more individualistic.

"My claim that women are relatively more communal and less agentic than men refers to a thematic difference between female and male behavior and not merely to differences in particular traits and behaviors. [-] In general, women are considerably more people oriented and less thing oriented than men" (*Alice H. Eagly, "The female psyche revisited: the importance of communion", The General Psychologist, June 2017*).

FEMININITY

Femininity is a set of qualities, behaviors and attributes regarded as characteristic of women and girls. Traditional feminine traits are gracefulness, empathy, gentleness, sensitivity, humility, dependence, tenderness, supportiveness... in opposition to traditional masculine traits which are aggressiveness, independence, dominance... All these are traditional gender stereotypes that sociologists often consider as socially constructed and not innate.

The French intellectual, Simone de Beauvoir, who influenced the second wave of feminists, stated that:

"One is not born, but rather becomes, a woman" (*Simone de Beauvoir, "The Second Sex"*).

In other words, she believed that femininity only results from a patriarchal and sexist discourse which, as a consequence, systematizes the subjugation and exploitation of women

"As patriarchy enforces a temperamental imbalance of personality traits between the sexes, its educational institutions, segregated or co-educational, accept a cultural programing toward the generally operative division between 'masculine' and 'feminine' subject matter, assigning the humanities and certain social sciences -at least in their lower or marginal branches- to the female, and science and technology, the professions, business and engineering to the male", (*Kate Millet, "Sexual Politics"*).

Then, what? Should we conclude that femininity is an abstract construction and that, apart from the physiological differences, there is nothing innate that would be intrinsically typical in the behavioral or psychological characteristic of females or males? That would be absurd! If it is difficult to say precisely which gender stereotype are innate or not, we can postulate without risk that both social and biological influences interact to shape feminine and masculine attributes

(*Richard A. Lippa, "Gender, Nature, and Nurture",
Psychology Press*).

Femininity is not just a construction to subjugate
women and girls! Femininity is not incompatible with
feminism and women empowerment. Quite the
contrary! Femininity is part of our very nature, of our
identity, of our whole being! Though it refers to the
social roles, behavior, and meanings prescribed to
women in society, and even if it is partly -or largely-
induced by society, it nevertheless constitutes a crucial
identifier essential to our existence as social animals,
specifically since the survival of our species depends
on sexual reproduction and not binary fission like cells
and other primitive life forms. Femininity, like
masculinity, contributes to shaping our individual
identity. And without identity, there is no real
existence. Our identity is both what makes us unique
and what permits us to communicate and live
together.

Hence, Femininity is an essential constituting element
of any girl and women. Of course, each of us live our
femininity differently; depending on our education,
family, culture... we will feel it and live it in our own

way. But the thing is: it is part of us! Every female, willingly or not, is feminine: there is something in our psyche, in our behavior, in our emotional lives that characterizes our gender and that is typical to our sex. Something that we all share if we are a girl or a woman. And the explanation is not exclusively of a sociological nature. There is something innate that characterizes females, which feeds their natural sense of otherness and caring...

*

New research shows that there are very few differences between men's and women's brains. Dr. Lise Eliot, neuroscientist at Rosalind Franklin University of Medicine and Science, who conducted a meta-synthesis of three decades of research, states that:

> "Men and women's brains do differ slightly, but the key finding is that these distinctions are due to brain size, not sex or gender". "Sex differences in the brain are tiny and inconsistent, once individuals' head size is accounted for. Sex differences are sexy, but this false impression that

there is such a thing as a 'male brain' and a 'female brain' has had wide impact on how we treat boys and girls, men and women". "The truth is that there are no universal, species-wide brain features that differ between the sexes. Rather, the brain is like other organs, such as the heart and kidneys, which are similar enough to be transplanted between women and men quite successfully." (*"Massive study reveals few differences between men and women's brains", EurekAlert*).

In other words, women and men have the same brain capacity. Therefore, if there are any innate differences opposing the two sexes, where do they come from? Are there any biological differences that could be identified as the true cause or source of the psycho-emotional distinctions that separate females and males? Dr. Louann Brizendine, from Langley Porter Psychiatric Institute in San Francisco -UCSF- says that the human female brain is affected by hormones, mostly estrogen -which is responsible for female physical features and reproduction- and progesterone (*Louann Brizendine, "The Female Brain*).

Estrogen, also known as the female hormone, is released by the ovaries and is a crucial element of the development of breasts, pubic hair, and the widening of the hips. In addition to regulating a female's periods, estrogen is also involved in bone formation, blood clotting, and the health of the skin and nails. It is such an essential 'regulator' in females' lives that we just can't ignore its emotional and psychological consequences! For instance, a depletion in estrogen, may induce low moods or depression. When estrogen levels fluctuate, as they do during menopause, women may experience hot flashes, low libido, and weight gain.

"Women and men use their brains differently. For example, different levels of estrogen, cortisol and dopamine [says Dr. Louann Brizendine] can cause a female to be more stressed by emotional conflict than her male counterpart. A few unpaid bills can set off a cascade of hormones in a woman that can catapult her into a fear of impending catastrophe, a reaction triggered in men only by physical danger. Women have 11 percent more neurons in the area of the brain devoted to emotions and memory. Because they have more "mirror neurons" they are also better at observing emotions in others", (*Julie Scelfo, "Why Girls Will Be Girls"*).

Dr. Louann Brizendine also insists on the differences in the architecture of the brain -prefrontal cortex, hypothalamus, amygdala- that regulates hormones and neurotransmitters, and identifies some minor differences, such as the fact that the part of the brain that weighs options and makes decisions is larger in women than men; the prefrontal cortex -which regulates emotions- and the insula -which plays a role in a variety of homeostatic functions related to basic survival needs, such as taste, visceral sensation, and autonomic control- are larger in women, such as the hippocampus -responsible for memory. Thus, women are, on average, better at expressing emotions and remembering the details of emotional events (*Louann Brizendine, "The Female Brain"*).

Women are clearly more emotional than men, indeed! But it is not a weakness! They are more caring, their sense of otherness is bigger and they are on average less aggressive... these are all qualities that appear to be necessary in social life!

INTERNATIONAL RELATIONS AND SECURITY

Although both genders are intellectually similar, because of their emotional differences, they nevertheless perceive the world differently and consequently the two sexes have diverging centers of interest and behavior. Therefore, the question could be: what might the world look like if we made women's concerns central?

We live in a man's world, made by and for men. Our societies have traditionally been governed by men, and we suffer the consequences of their psychological and emotional bias and shortcomings. The use of force and aggression were and -way too often- remain a constant rule characterizing not only local and national politics, but international politics too. Societies and the International System were built on masculinist notions of Human Nature, which is here seen through a Hobbesian perspective -a war of everyone against everyone since the essence of human nature is perceived as being selfish and aggressive-, hence perpetuating insecurity. No nation can survive if it is not prepared to go to war; and of course, such a perspective creates a circular problem whereby when one state steps up its military capabilities, others see it as a threat and consequently do their best to heighten their own security, generating at best an arms race and at worst an escalation that might easily lead to an open conflict.

"Masculinity and politics have a long and close association. Characteristics associated with 'manliness' such as toughness, courage, power, independence, and even physical strength, have, throughout history, been those most valued in the conduct of politics, particularly international politics. Frequently, manliness has also been associated with violence and the use of force, a type of behavior that, when conducted in the international arena, has been valorized and applauded in the name of defending one's country" (*J. Ann Tickner, "Gender in International*

Relations: Feminist Perspectives on Achieving Global Security).

*

The feminist contribution to the study of International Relations and Security is not limited to the recognition that IR have long been appropriated by men. It also adds to a redefinition of the concept of security, which must be seen in a broader and multidimensional perspective that goes beyond the security of states and includes various issues such as: the use of sexual violence as a tool of war in conflict; poverty; gender subordination; human trafficking; ecological devastation... which can all contribute to social destabilization and further insecurity.

Obviously, the classical patriarchal 'Realist' vision of International Relations is insufficient -and irrelevant- to give a clear and holistic understanding of the world and the stakes that threatens its existence. Hence, there is an absolute need to include new perspectives, including gender issues in the study of International Relations to come to more realistic perspectives:

"Many of the things that we take for granted - among them security- could not exist in their current form without gender hierarchy. For example, the international political economy is reliant on taking women's unpaid labor for granted (and thus entrenching gender subordination). Similarly, international security practice often relies on the invisibility of women (both as labor and as a casus belli) specifically and gender generally" (Laura Sjoberg, "Introduction to Security Studies: Feminist Contributions").

*

More importantly, however, empowering women - that is to say: ending every discrimination to give equal chances and opportunities to both sexes- would contribute to promote international stability and peace efficiently!

Firstly, because this could help reduce the weight and consequences of the masculine psychological bias that fosters competition and aggressiveness in a world which is becoming extremely complex and where the interconnections and resulting interdependences call for improved collaboration and enhanced multi-lateralism. Indeed, considering that females are less inclined towards violence and aggression and are more caring, co-operative and communal, the feminization of societies -or women empowerment- could be seen as a direct contribution to secure world stability and peace.

Secondly, securing gender economic, social and political equality would certainly contribute to reducing the social divide and poverty that weakens societies, especially regarding developing countries. It is indeed urgent to understand that, instead of making societies stronger, the exclusion or marginalization of women and girls doesn't help societies do their best and inevitably constricts their potential. Poverty -in every sense of the word: economic, cultural, environ-mental…- and wealth gaps corrode the underpinnings of free society and human progress. When a society is weak, its ability to respond to crisis situation is undermined; yet, we know that we will all have to face important and extremely complex challenges in the future, due to the emerging global risks -climate change, pandemics, lack of resources, etc… And since progress feeds improved connections and inter-dependences -symbolized by the notion of 'Global Village'-, instability somewhere might harm the whole international system. Hence, empowering women is not only a way to make societies more efficient, but a necessity to reduce the gaps that feed the instabilities which will make the world increasingly unsafe if we do not care.

WOMEN AND DEVELOPMENT

Until the XXth century, women's involvement in the economy was essentially -if not exclusively- seen as informal and limited to their domestic roles of mothers and wives. Their economic activity was spatially restricted to their household -private sphere- and was related primarily to the reproductive function. It was only in 1970 that Esther Boserup, a Danish economist, suggested that women should be considered as agents of development and modernization. In other words -and by extension-, she postulated that encouraging gender equality would help boost economic efficiency (*Esther Boserup, "Women's Role in Economic Development"*).

Boserup also stated that increased education for women in the developing world could reduce family size, which in turn could help to reduce poverty. Educating women and girls in developing countries could have an enormous impact on these societies since better educated women would earn a higher income and would be more likely to buy more goods and services, hence stimulating demand... and production. Better educated women would also make an additional workforce to the strategic sectors of production; they would help grow Research and Development, and competitiveness. And of course, because they would need to work to keep up their standard of living, they would reduce their fertility.

And, what is true for developing nations is true for every nation, every economy:

> "Economies are more resilient, productive and inclusive when they reduce gender inequalities and actively support the equal participation of women in all spheres of life" (*"Gender and development"*, OECD).

*

The concept of 'Sustainable Development' emerged in the late 1980s from the report 'Our Common Future' published by the U.N. World Commission on Environment and Development. Sustainable Development is seen as a strategy for development that meets the needs of the present without compromising the ability of future generations to meet their own needs (*"Sustainable Development". UNESCO. 3 August 2015*). And of course, women have an important role to play here:

> "Women have a vital role in environmental management and development. Their full participation is therefore essential to achieve sustainable development", (Principle 20 of the Rio Declaration). _ "By providing the same opportunities to women and men, including in decision-making in all kinds of activities, a sustainable path of development can be achieved to ensure that women's and men's interests are both taken into account in the allocation of resources" (*"Empowering Women for Sustainable Deve-lopment", United Nations Economic Commission for Europe*).

We cannot afford to miss the path of sustainable development. If we do, this will mean the total destruction of resources, many of which are not renewable or recyclable, and consequently this would lead to the destruction of our civilization. The participation of women, the participation of everyone is needed: to produce, to innovate, to find the strategies and knowledge that will help to produce differently, in a more eco-friendly and socially responsible way. Although it is easy to understand that we need everyone, that we cannot afford to exclude or marginalize whole segments of the community; we should not forget that if we do not give equal opportunities to include everyone nothing will be possible!

It is indeed essential to invest massively in the education of girls and women. And to do so, we must break the social barriers and stereotypes which dampen their ascension; we must create a safer environment so that no one is tempted to hide in fear of being a victim of abuse.

Furthermore, enhancing women's education and health would improve child health and survival; indeed, educated mothers -and fathers- are more likely to seek immunizations for their children, provide better nutrition, and thereby improve the survival chances of their children. In addition, if mothers had more control over their lives they would be less likely to experience domestic violence; hence their children would be less likely to be exposed to violence in the home, which in turn would reduce the likelihood of lifetime adverse consequences from this exposure for the next generation.

"Greater control over household resources by women leads to more investment in children's human capital, with dynamic positive effects on economic growth" ("World Development Report 2012: Gender Equality and Development", World Bank Group).

*

One cannot grow if we do not grow together; and the actual situation is certainly not satisfying!

"Women who predominate among the world's poor are at greater risk of environmental challenges as they often lack the necessary means to successfully adapt and protect themselves"

There is indeed an urgent need to help women and girls improve their status and living standards. It is in interest of both women and men because it is the only way to preserve stability and peace for future generations.

However, as explained above, this will not be possible if we do not fight against stereotypes to open the doors and give girls and women access to every sector of activity. That is precisely the objectives of the Gender and Development -GAD- strategy, an approach which was developed in the 1980s with the catalyst of the United Nations as an alternative to the Women In Development approach -WID. The idea is to improve the model of development by removing disparities in the social, economic, and political balances between women and men as a pre-condition for achieving people-centred development.

"Women's disadvantaged position is also a result of the way the economic system recreates gender inequalities and precarious types of employment, thereby raising questions about the type of development that women are to be integrated in" (*Lourdes Beneria & al, "Gender Development and Globalization: - Economics, as if All People Mattered"*).

In other words, this approach focuses on the gendered division of labor and on the way societies assign roles, responsibilities and expectations to both women and men. GAD policies aim to break the boundaries which exclude women from certain lines of business and decision-making positions in order to keep them in their domestic role. It denounces the oppression of women in the family or private sphere and in society, insisting on the fact that women are agents of change and development, and not just passive recipients of development.

*

"We have moved from viewing women as victims to seeing them as essential to finding solutions to the world's problems", Speaker at the UN Conference on Women, Beijing 1995, (*Lourdes*

Beneria & al, Gender, "Development and Globalization...").

Women's economic activities, their ability to work in any sector of the economy, and hence their contribution to society, depend on their integration or on their marginalization within the said community, which are conditioned by the norms and stereotypes that frame the society. In other words, if empowering women -that is to say to give them access to every sector, every level of responsibility, with the same pay and status as men working in the same conditions- is necessary to ensure a safe future for Mankind, the fundamentals of society must change by discarding patriarchy.

Preventing women of having equal access to the public sphere and to the labor market has been -and often remains- the norm for patriarchy. But we should now be aware that, though it is obviously a relic of the past, it still exists and could prove to be extremely harmful for the future of our societies. Indeed, we should understand that if women and girls cannot contribute satisfyingly to the development of our societies, it is the whole species that might suffer the consequences.

In other words, because it inhibits development, patriarchy threatens both men and women.

PART 3

<u>WOMEN'S PRIDE</u>

Throughout history, women and girls have been subjected to all sorts of abuse, sexual violence, and domestic cruelty. They have been treated as mere objects, seen as the property of their male relatives, excluded from the public sphere; they have been denied the right to education and considered as irresponsible and inferior creatures. They have spent most of their lives secluded and have been denied the essentials of a life of dignity. They were also often undernourished, especially when compared to their male relatives, and have lived in precarious conditions. Baby-girls have often been victims of infanticide -and still are today in some places! And when they were given a chance to live, they were forced to marry at a very young age with a man they didn't choose; a man who, most of the time, they didn't know… and this is sadly still the case today in some regions.

Women have been denied fundamental human rights. They have been humiliated, abused, victimised, marginalized… and all this, from a very young age:

"Euripides shows us women victimized by patriarchy in almost every possible way. A girl needs both her virginity and a dowry to attract a husband. Women are raped and bear illegitimate children whom they must discard. The women are blamed, while the men who raped them are not. When marriages prove to be unfruitful, wives are inevitably guilty. Despite the grimness of marriage, spinster-hood is worse…" (*Sarah B Pomeroy, "Goddesses, Wives and Slaves*).

Since the earliest civilisations, and maybe even before, men have constantly argued that females are psychologically, intellectually, emotionally ... inferior to males; they have insisted that women are sinful, lecherous, that they are filthy 'creatures'. They have affirmed that we are intrinsically immature -which, in some ways, is not entirely false considering that girls have been forced to marry when they were only 13 or 14 years old to men who were 20 or 30 years older than them. They have proclaimed that we are an unfinished version of man who is supposedly a 'Godlike' perfection! Of course!!

In ancient Greece, they were even deprived of their parenthood since their contribution to conception was seen as being exclusively passive: they only were the 'receptacles for the father's seed':

> "She who is called the mother is not her offspring's parent, but nurse to the newly sown embryo. The male _who mounts_ begets. The female, a stranger" (*Aeschylus, "Eumenides", 658, quoted by: Sarah B Pomeroy, "Goddesses, Wives and Slaves*).

Chinese traditional philosophy assimilates the 'Yin' as the female principle; it represents darkness, femininity, passivity, and the earth; on the contrary, the 'Yang' or male principle, represents the sun, light, masculinity, activity, and the heavens! (*"Gender in Chinese Philosophy", Internet Encyclopedia of Philosophy*).

But they were all wrong!!! In spite of the discredit and disdain, and despite the physical and emotional pain they suffered -and still suffer-, women and girls don't have to feel ashamed! Quite the contrary, they should be proud of who they are and what they have done! Against all odds, they've been able to survive the ignominious treatments which have been imposed on them! They have shown great resilience and strength; one might ask whether men would have had the same capacity of resilience! It is indeed easier to impose your will and whims when you are in a position of strength, than bearing a burden of injustice and oppression! Deprived of everything, muzzled, sometimes beaten, objectified, secluded... women nevertheless have managed to survive and to raise their children. Lately, as they have gained access to education and the economy, they have kept their traditional tasks while given more responsibilities to become an essential constituent part of the many dimensions of society: the economy, culture, science and politics... even if they are still way too often victims of discrimination and abuse.

Women and girls have bravely proven they are in no way inferior to men and boys! The real question is: who should be ashamed? The historical victim or the long-term abuser?

<u>'X' IS THE 'FIRST' SEX</u>

It is now time to take a different perspective to prove once and for all that, in spite of the patriarchal tyranny, females are certainly not inferior to males and that there is no reason to be ashamed of being a woman nor to restrain our ambitions. First things first, females and males are two necessary components of sexual reproduction. Without the existence of females it would be impossible for sexually reproducing creatures to have offspring and perpetuate the species. It is as simple as that!

Sexual reproduction is of course not the only mode of reproduction; it's a product of evolution which emerged after asexual reproduction. The latter only needs one parent and might take different forms: binary fission -the parent cell doubles its DNA and divides into two similar cells, which is the mode of reproduction used by bacteria; fragmentation, when the parent organism breaks into fragments or pieces and each fragment develops into a new individual; budding, when the parent organism develops an outgrowth or bud which ultimately becomes a new individual after maturity; and parthenogenesis: in this case, the embryo develops without fertilization by sperm, which is the case for invertebrates, as well as in some fish, amphibians, and reptiles.

Except in the case of hermaphroditism, where one individual owns both sexes, sexual reproduction requires two parents who combine their genes to make an offspring:

> "Sex is recombination plus outcrossing. [-] Sex equals genetic mixing [which] is good for evolution because it helps create variety. [-] Sex is a sort of free trade in good genetic inventions and thus greatly increases the chances that they will spread through a species and the species will evolve" (*Matt Ridley, "The Red Queen. Sex and Evolution of Human Nature"*).

In other words, sexual reproduction is a strategy which stimulates genetic variety to improve resilience and adaptation. Hence, the two sex chromosomes of both parents -XX for the mother, and XY for the Father- combine to make an offspring who will either be a female -who will then inherit the X of her mother and the X of her father- or a male -with the X of his mother and Y of his father.

*

Uneducated macho men and simple-minded archaic misogynists will of course say that the fact that males have two different chromosomes X and Y while females only have two Xs proves that the former are more sophisticated and complex than the latter who are unsophisticated compared to males, and monotonous, hence proving the 'natural' superiority of males over females. But they are wrong! If we take a closer look and compare the X and Y chromosomes, we will see that the X is far more sophisticated than the Y, and that a XX is certainly not a poor combination compared to the XY; quite the contrary!

The Y chromosome, or 'male' chromosome, is one third the size of the X, or 'female' chromosome. The Y likely contains 50 to 60 genes while the X chromosome contains about 900 genes and is consequently way much bigger in density and information (*"12 Neat Facts about the Y Chromosome"*; and: *"X Chromosome", National Human Genome Research Institute*). Actually, the Y chromosome, which now contains only 3 percent of the genes that it once shared with the X chromosome, is seen by scientists as undergoing a rapid evolutionary deterioration (*Roseanne F. Zhao, "The Y chromosome: beyond gender determination", National Human Genome Research Institute*).

> "Y chromosomes are genetically degenerate, having lost most of the active genes that were present in their ancestors" (B. Charlesworth, D. Charlesworth, "The degeneration of Y chromosomes", National Center for Biotechnology Information, U.S. National Library of Medicine).

Consequently, many more genes are strung along the XX female chromosome -2x900- than in the XY male chromosome -900+55. Hence, contrary to what Aeschylus and ancient Greeks thought, mothers are clearly the parents of their offspring! Even more: if a girl has the same number of genes coming from their father and from their mother -the X of their father + the X of their mother = 2x 900-, boys are genetically closer to their mother than to their father -the X of their mother = 900 genes, + the Y of their father = 55.

"A son, in fact, may rightfully be thought of as a mama's boy: he has ~~he~~ X chromosome alive in every cell of his body. He has no choice – it's the only X he's got, and every cell needs it. Thus, he has more of his mother's genes operating in his body than he does of his father's" (*Natalie Angier, "WOMAN. An intimate Geography"*).

THE SMART CHROMOSOME

If the X chromosome has long been considered as an element that has hardly changed since the pre-mammal days when it was a part of another 'autosome' pair -asexual chromosomes-, it appears that compared to the genetically impoverished Y chromosome, the X with its multitude of genes can be considered as the Smart Chromosome. Indeed, the X carries intelligence genes and is involved in the development of the brain; and since women have two Xs, they are more likely to transmit intelligence genes to their children. In addition to this, it is now believed that genes for advanced cognitive functions which are inherited from the father may be automatically deactivated (*J. Graves, J. Gecz, H. Hameister, "Evolution of the human X – a smart and sexy chromosome that controls speciation and development", National Center for Biotechnology Information, U.S. National Library of Medicine, 2002;* and: *Charlotte England, "Children inherit their intelligence from their mother not their father, say scientists"*).

As explained above, the Y chromosome is small and contains only a few genes which are essentially used to produce sperm and the SRY gene which provides instructions for making a protein called the sex-determining region Y protein, involved in male-typical sex development. On the contrary the huge X chromosome contains a multitude of genes which, for most of them, determine a great variety of proteins involved in an equally wide variety of metabolic functions and are not involved in sexual differentiation. Hence, the X chromosome is essential to life for both males and females. For its part, however, the Y chromosome only serves to determine the making of a male.

The fact that males only have one X might also explain why women outlive men everywhere in the world - except in ancient times when ill-treatment, abuse, pregnancy and childbirth were the principal causes of death for women. Indeed, the complexity of the X and its multitude of genes and their importance to secure metabolic functions, can sometimes cause genetic dysfunctions and pathologies; but because they have two Xs, females have some sort of possible back-up to override these dysfunctions and pathologies. Males don't.

> "Men don't have a back-up. If anything goes wrong with their X chromosome, they are in trouble. That puts them at risk of genetic diseases that can shorten their lifespans" (*Liam Mannix, "X is greater than Y: Chromosomes may explain why women outlive men"*).

Now, if someone wonders which of the two sexes is the weaker, we should answer with certitude that this is certainly not the female!

*

Last, but not least, the participation of the X is also required for fetal sex determination! When the testes of a male fetus bud, they start producing testosterone, an androgen -sex hormone- responsible for the normal evolution of males: the female program enshrined in the male fetus is then inhibited by a hormone called

Müllerian Inhibiting Factor -MIF-; without that, the evolution of the fetus would keep the shape of a female. In other words, androgens are essential to prevent the development of the Müllerian ducts in the uterus and fallopian tubes and permit the development of male genitalia and the masculinization of the body. Without this intervention, evolution of the fetus, either XX or XY, would take a feminine direction, even if some major female characteristics are missing. Hence, in the case of MIF dysfunction with a XY fetus, we might have an embryonic testes and penis, and the absence of Fallopian tubes… followed by an interruption of the process of masculinization with the development of a short vagina, breasts… In other words, an XY fetus needs the X gene to become truly male.

> "Persistent Müllerian duct syndrome type 1, a disorder of sexual development that affects males, is caused by mutations in the AMH gene. Males with this condition have female reproductive organs in addition to normal male reproductive organs" (*"AMH gene", Medline Plus, National Library of Medicine*).

To sum up, let's insist on the following conclusive remarks. Firstly the female program is present in every mammal fetus, XX or XY! And in case of dysfunction of the process of masculinization of a XY fetus the evolutionary model will follow the female pattern which is preserved in each of us. Secondly, the male needs the female in any case because he is partly X. What is more, the XY fetus is not capable of securing the genetic mutation that turns him into a male in the absence of X, whereas the XX has no male feature and doesn't need any to become a female. Why then consider that she is the lesser sex? She is not! And if we want to play this game, we'd better say that she is the greater sex. Chronologically and genetically!

> "By the conventional reckoning of embryology, females are said to be the 'default' or 'neutral' sex, males the 'organized' or activated' sex. That is, a fetus will grow into a girl in the absence of fetal hormones" (*Natalie Angier, "Woman"*).

There are no females with a Y chromosome and no males that don't have an X chromosome, and contrary to the X, the Y does not contain certain genes necessary for the mammal's survival.

At present, the two sex chromosomes are thought to have evolved from a pair of autosomes in an ancestral mammal. One of them has been altered and became known as the Y chromosome while the remaining autosome became the sex chromosome X. In other words, the X is the original version and the Y is a derived and impoverished version.

> "The two X chromosomes inherited by females look nearly identical to the other non-sex chromosomes, so-called autosomes. The Y chromosome, however, which is inherited by males in concert with one X chromosome, is a withered version of the X, having lost many genes since it stopped recombining with the X chromosome" (*"The Story Of X: Evolution Of A Sex Chromosome", Science Daily, April 2009*).

Hence, we could conclude that if -as it is today almost universally admitted- women do not come from Adam's rib... it would therefore not be totally unwise, given the conclusions of recent discoveries about our chromosomes, to argue that men come from Eve's rib!

PART 4

<u>BEHIND THE PARADOXICAL SOCIAL AND INTELLECTUAL INSIGNIFICANCE OF WOMEN THROUGHOUT HISTORY</u>

According to the above analysis, there is no reason for girls and women to be seen or treated as if they were inferior to boys and men. There is no evidence of intrinsic female inferiority or male superiority. However, Human females have long been objectified and socially, politically, psychologically, economically and physically dominated by their male counterparts! How come? Why?

Paradoxically, since the most ancient times, women were given utmost importance in poetry and fiction:

> "Women have burnt like beacons in all the works of all poets from the beginning of times – Clytemnestra, Antigone, Cleopatra, Lady Macbeth, Phedre, Cressida, Rosalind, Desdemona, the Duchess of Malfi, among the dramatists; then among the prose writers: Millamant, Clarissa, Becky Sharp, Anna Karenina, Emma Bovary, Madame de Germantes – the names flock to mind, nor do they recall women 'lacking in personality and character'" (*Virginia Woolf, "A room of One's Own"*).

As Virginia Woolf puts it, in the realm of fiction women can be heroic and mean, splendid and sordid, infinitely beautiful and hideous in the extreme, great as the greatest among men. But that was only possible in fiction! And even there, their 'existence' and importance was only seen 'by men' and always in relation to men. However, even if they equaled and surpassed men in fiction... in the real-world women remained insignificant and were forbidden to express themselves, isolated in the private sphere, forced to remain submissive to men.

One of the keys of their social inexistence throughout history was that, until recently -late XVIIIth, XIXth, and even XXth centuries-, women were given no time, no place, no opportunity or possibility to express themselves, to learn, to write, to get any experience of the real world, or to create. They were secluded, excluded from the world and trapped in a 'tiny cage'. They were given no chances to grow, kept and owned like pets and prevented from thinking, creating, or governing their own lives.

Western societies have long excluded women from theoretical and scientific knowledge -which was considered inherently 'masculine'-, hence preventing women from acquiring and producing anything that could free them and lead them to power. To this end, they pretended that knowledge would divert women's vital energies from their 'natural' reproductive function (*Elizabeth Anderson, "Feminist epistemology: An interpretation and a defense Elizabeth Anderson"*).

And in so doing, they were able to keep women and girls trapped in a cage of ignorance and inferiority, two essential conditions to subdue them and keep total control over their lives and condition of existence. Furthermore, since as far back as we can remember women and girls have always been obliged to remain cloistered and to comply with their male counterparts' desires and authority, their position of inferiority and submission was seen as natural and inevitable.

*

Even after women and girls were given access to education and science, androcentrism continued to taint every discipline and every scientific research, from biology to social sciences and literary studies:

> "Theories take males, men's lives, or 'masculinity' to set the norm for humans or animals generally, with female differences either ignored or represented as deviant" (*Elizabeth Anderson, "Feminist epistemology: An interpretation and a defense"*).

In a man's world, the norm had to be masculine! Everything feminine was inferior, biased, improper, divergent, or dangerously digressive. Knowledge leads to power, and it had to remain in men's hands!

Fortunately, things have changed slightly during the last decades. Nevertheless, androcentrism remains the core axis governing science in many areas: according to UNESCO, in 2016 women accounted for only 29.3% of the world's scientific researchers (*"Women in Science", UNESCO*). This discrimination against women in science, and against everything that is feminine, explains for instance why it is that there is still better knowledge and understanding of the Y chromosome than the X, even if the latter is obviously more complex and determinative. It is why the dominant theories in International Relations -the so called 'Realist' school of thought- consider and see as a constant the fact that men's supposedly typical traits, aggressiveness and selfishness, drive human behavior and international politics -thus leading to harsh competition, insecurity and militarization (*Jeffrey Haynes, Peter Hough…, "World Politics; International*

Relations and Globalization in the 21st Century"). It also explains why women have long been excluded from historical or anthropological research! In some ways, science excluded women from humanity. Or let's say it differently: the only acceptable scientific model to depict Humankind was masculine!

THE ESSENTIAL CONTRIBUTION OF WOMEN TO CONTEMPORARY SOCIETY

Unlike the above-mentioned once universally admitted postulate, the status imposed on women and girls -their alleged 'natural' inferiority and their consequential submission to males' rule- is not innate:

> « In our primal brain, the world is gynocentric. The great majority of Primate Species live in social groups, and the core of those groups is female » (*Natalie Angier, « Women »*).

Let us be clear: gynocentrism doesn't mean gynocracy. The fact that females assume key responsibilities in most Primate Communities, the fact that they don't necessarily let males take decisions regarding their infants or their daily existence doesn't mean that they rule over males. However, with the exception of

Chimpanzees and Gorillas, females play a central role in determining the social organization of primate species. In most multi-female groups of primates, females spend their lives in the group where they are born, so that different mothers and their offspring tend to be closely related. Breeding males, on the other hand, are normally outsiders who were born elsewhere.

Richard Wrangham, a prominent anthropologist and primatologist, argued that food allocation is a primary determinant of the distribution and grouping of females which in turn is the primary determinant of males mating strategies and the distribution of males (*"Advances in the Study of Behavior"*, *Vol. 22, Academic Press, San Diego, 1993: Peter J.B. Slater, Manfred Milinski, "Male Aggression and Sexual Coercion of Females in Non-Human Primates and other Mammals"*). In other words, the entire social organization and functioning depends on females!

Even regarding human societies, men's role has always been essentially connected to external activities: making war, settling community rules and policing the society... but social cohesion has been secured by women, who are the principal keepers of their household. When Athenian men were at war, women remained in the city and kept their household and by extension the city alive. In spite of their proclaimed mediocrity and insignificance, women's social role and their contribution to the existence and to the survival of their communities has always been essential!

We have already detailed how the positive contribution of women to keep social and world stability is crucial. At present, it is seen as such and proclaimed by the United Nations Organisation! Indeed, women and girls' daily activities have changed dramatically over the past decades… In fact, their tasks haven't just changed, but have multiplied! Indeed, they haven't abandoned their traditional occupations, such as housekeeping, caring and breeding their infants…; but have been given a multitude of new responsibilities and roles which, until recently, were exclusively reserved for men. The reason behind this transformation is that we live in a growing complex environment, and the contribution from just men would clearly be insufficient. Obviously, the greater participation of women constitutes an absolute necessity for modern societies. And the truth is: today, women's activities and responsibilities have multiplied, while men's have remained stable!

*

Let us briefly conclude from what was said above about the contribution of women to society: their contribution is not just important; it is crucial, surpassing that of men's. Women are still house-keepers and breeders, but they are also breadwinners. Apart from multitasking, they help society grow thanks to their contribution to the economy, to science, to culture and to the arts… They even outnumber men at universities (*Paulette Delgado, "Women Outnumber Men at a Record High at US Universities"; "Women Increasingly outnumber men at US colleges; but why?", Georgetown University;* and: *"Women in EU Outnumber Men as Students & Graduates at Bachelor's & Master's Levels", Schengenvisainfonews*).

According to the United Nations Economic Commission for Europe -UNECE-, more than 55 per cent of tertiary graduates are women in the 39 out of

47 UNECE countries with data ("*Women outnumber men in higher education but gender stereotyped subject choices persist*", UNECE). However, the report states that, if females outnumber males in higher education, their share has declined in many countries during the past decade.

Furthermore, several sectors like Communication Technologies -ICT- or Engineering, Manufacturing and Construction -EMC- remain mostly masculine, a segregation which is also due to employers.

In spite of the general improvement during the last decades and the growing participation of women in society, the overall situation remains fragile, and far from satisfactory!

WOMEN IN A MAN'S WORLD

The situation of women in the world is still extremely fragile, indeed. They need, among other things, easier access to essential services and rights. Way too often, they are the sole person responsible for the education and upbringing of their children. Paradoxically, their living conditions -wages, housing...- are often inadequate and their access to necessary services are insufficient. In other words, the equation between their contribution and their retribution is unbalanced and totally lopsided. Moreover, as explained above the distribution of wages and other benefits are still largely unequal.

Regarding higher education, even if women now outnumber men in colleges and universities in most advanced economies, gender parity remains acute in several disciplines:

"The subjects studied at tertiary level by women and men can reflect stereotypes of 'masculine' and 'feminine' subject areas" (*"Women outnumber men in higher education but gender stereotyped subject choices persist"*, UNECE).

As for their participation in politics, only 21 per cent of government ministers were women in September 2021, and only 14 countries have achieved 50 per cent or more women in cabinets. With an annual increase of just 0.52 percentage points, gender parity in ministerial positions will not be achieved before 2077 (*"Facts and figures: Women's leadership and political participation"*, UNWomen). And it is not surprising that the five most commonly held portfolios by women ministers are: family / children / youth / elderly / disabled!

The current global labour force participation rate for women is just under 47%, while it is 72% for men, a difference of 25 percentage points, with some regions facing a gap of more than 50 percentage points (*"The gender gap in employment: What's holding women back?"*, ILO). Indeed, it is more difficult for women to find a job than for men. Furthermore, women tend to be overrepresented in vulnerable jobs, hence exacerbating their economic and social precariousness. Even regarding the proportion of women in business senior management around the globe, women hold only 32% of top leadership positions in 2022 (*"Women now hold 32% of top leadership positions", Grant Thornton*).

Worse! We still suffer violence from perverts like Harvey Weinstein and world leaders like Donald Trump or Vladimir Putin who have done their best to restore the most abject form of discrimination against women. For instance, although domestic violence is endemic in Russia, the Russian government adopted a new law in 2017 stipulating that domestic violence that results in 'minor harm' such as small lacerations and bruising, be considered a misdemeanor punishable by a fine of up to $500 or up to 15 days in jail (*"Vladimir Putin Just Signed Off on the Partial Decriminalization of Domestic Abuse in Russia", Time Magazine*). In America, during his five years mandate, Donald Trump harmed women's rights in several ways: he threatened private abortion rights, he undermined easy access to health care -ACA-, and he removed key non-discriminatory protections in health care. He also contributed to eroding equal pay by discontinuing pay data collection; he dismantled the family planning network, and he put female students at greater risk of sexual harassment and assault with the change of Title IX of the Education Amendments of 1972 (*"Women have paid the price for Trump's Regulatory Agenda"*, *CAP*). These aberrant decisions were taken in the twenty-first century by the governments of two of the most powerful countries and, sadly, they are not the only devastating policies taken by modern governments!

Last but not least, as shown by the Russian invasion of Ukraine or by the many conflicts around the world, women are the principal victims of war. Since they are the primary caregivers in many societies, women are particularly hit by the economic consequences of war and its destruction and spoliation of resources; they are also often victims of sexual violence, even more so since rape is part of the strategy of fear and social destruction.

"Traditionally, as they are more likely to be involved in direct combat, men have made up the main casualties of war. However, in recent times it is women and children who have been more likely to be affected as civilian casualties have dramatically risen from about 10 percent at the beginning of the twentieth century to around 90 percent by the end of the century" (*"J. Haynes, P. Hough..., "World Politics; International Relations and Globalization in the 21st Century"*).

Furthermore, if women are often the direct victims of direct aggression, they are also indirect victims when they are left alone with their children after the death or the disappearance of their husbands (*"Women and War: Women & Armed Conflicts and the issue of Sexual Violence", ISS-ICRC*). But if they suffer the atrocities of war, they also suffer its long-term consequences; for instance, when infrastructures are devastated, when the economy is gravely disrupted, and when as a result the school system is not working satisfyingly, girls are disproportionally affected in their right to education.

<u>THE ABSTRUSE DOMINATION OF MAN</u>

The analysis above shows that men are not intrinsically superior to women. So, how come they have imposed their domination?

Throughout recorded history, men have been driven by a quest for power, and they have succeeded thanks to strategies of coalition. In other words, the power of one man depends on other men!

Men's rule was made by and for men; it required the support of other men. While confining women to the private domestic domain, excluding them from the public sphere to isolate them, men were communicating and cooperating together! The alliance of men was secured against women! In other words, in spite of their division, the realm of men made necessary the union of men to keep the realm of women fragmented… Women and girls seclusion, the deprivation of their fundamental rights required that men join forces to control them and strengthen their power.

Yes! It is the seclusion of women which contributed to their marginalisation and consequently to their subordination! Excluding women from public life contributed to debar them from power, subjecting them de facto to male domination. This is especially true considering that men's quest for power ultimately meant securing sexual control over women:

> "Men would treat Power not as an end in itself, but as a means to sexual reproductive success" (*Matt Ridley, "The Red Queen"*).

It is widely admitted that male aggression against females in primates, including humans, often functions to control female sexuality to the male's reproductive advantage. In so doing, he secures or tries to secure the survival of his genes (*Barbara Smuts, "Male Aggression against Women: An Evolutionary Perspective"*).

*

Evolutionary Psychology and 'common knowledge' postulate that in the Homo genus, the two sexes share different characteristics and priorities: men place a greater value on signs of fertility -such as youth- and sexual fidelity -such as coyness-, while women place a greater value on signs of a lifelong provider -status, strength, devotion (*Robert Wright, "The Moral Animal: Why We Are the Way We Are: The New Science of Evolutionary Psychology"*).

In other words, the domination of men over women came supposedly from the latter's will to secure protection from a strong and powerful mate capable of defending her offspring in case of external aggression. Indeed, since they give birth to immature and defenseless children who require an extremely long period of parent caring -leaving their mothers more insecure than females of other species-, females belonging to the genus Homo sacrifice their independence for security, unlike most other primates. In other words, the domination of men over women has come 'naturally', and consequently women are seen as being responsible for their situation!

Quoting Patricia Gowaty, from UCLA, Natalie Angier proposed another scenario:

> "The 'Good Genes' model leads to oversimplified notions that there is a 'best male' out there, a top of the line hunk whom all females would prefer to mate with if they had the wherewithal. But in the viability model, a female brings her own genetic complement in the equation, with the result that what looks good genetically to one woman might be a clash of colors for another" (*Natalie Angier, "Women. An Intimate Geography"*).

There are indeed differences opposing women and we are not all programmed to look for the same 'Alpha male'. And this is fortunate! We are not robots, but emotional individuals. Despite sharing common characteristics, each of us is equipped with our own genetic background, emotions, and needs. What is beautiful or what might constitute a priority for one of us can be perceived differently by another woman. Women do not necessarily choose their mates because they are the strongest, or because they are powerful. There are other criteria that determine their choice -when they are given the opportunity to choose!

Women in general do not seek to be dominated, to be victimised and to be treated like mere objects. They didn't come into life to be controlled and owned by men! They are not predestined to submit, to suffer, to be inferior and to belong to the opposite sex. They are not intrinsically coy and obedient animals. They are not insignificant beings, even if this is what we have been told; quite the contrary! It is explained above: their contribution to social stability has always been essential. How then can we explain their situation? What are the origins of Patriarchy?

ORIGINS OF PATRIARCHY

Gerda Lerner defines patriarchy as:

"The manifestation and institutionalization of male dominance over women and children in the family and the extension of male dominance over women in society in general" (*Gerda Lerner, "The Creation of Patriarchy"*).

Rejecting the idea that female domination is natural and universal, Gerda Lerner insists that hunter-gatherer societies are egalitarian as male and female functions complement one another and the relative status of the sexes is 'separate but equal'. The '!Kung' people of the Kalahari Desert in Southern Africa are often quoted as an example: while men tend to hunt and women tend to gather, these roles often overlap. Women retain control over the food they gather. Both men and women raise children equally (*Patricia Draper, "!Kung Women: Contrasts in Sexual Egalitarianism in Foraging and Sedentary Contexts"*).

Inequality and the domination of women by men most probably came during the Neolithic as a result of the Agricultural revolution, which started 12,000 years ago and imposed a sexual division of labor based on physical strength, reflecting the reproductive differences that separate the two sexes and confined women to their childbearing and childrearing capacities. Indeed, traditional farming activities are labor intensive and require strength; ploughing requires significant upper-body strength, grip strength, and is hardly compatible with childcare which has remained the responsibility of women (*Esther Boserup, "Women's Role in Economic Development"*). Further-more, the development of resources produced by agriculture had to be defended, strengthening the importance of physically stronger males.

Thus, labor roles became more gendered: while men did the majority of-fieldwork, women were relegated to child-rearing and household work. Hence, without contributing to food production, they lost control over resources and became second-class citizens. However, since they remained essential for the survival of the species, as reproducers, they were a vital resource that men needed and wanted to own in order to ensure their lineage. Furthermore, if like contemporary hunter-gatherer societies such as the !Kung, pre-Neolithic communities were matrilocal - daughters remained with their mother after marriage-, things changed with the Agricultural revolution and the growing importance of men's contribution to resource production: property was now passed down the male line and societies became patrilocal. And as young women were forced to leave their parents to settle with their husband, they lost their autonomy, they lost their bearings, their connections, and found themselves entirely dependent. They lost control over everything, even over their body, to become at best child bearer, when they were not enslaved and raped to satisfy men's greedy pleasures.

Being both attractive and subordinate, they became the victims of a society of double standards, forced to suffer all sorts of abuse and humiliation; and that was true for women of every social class. Gender inequality was everywhere. If wives had to obey their husband and were excluded from the public sphere, women slaves suffered the dishonor of being sexually used by their master -something that was usually not experienced by male slaves (*Gerda Lerner, "The Creation of Patriarchy"*). In essence, being a female meant being inferior, owned, controlled... abused one way or another.

Religions too participated in and strengthened the process of male dominance. As explained before, male Gods began to strip Goddesses of their power by the late Neolithic; then, the emergence of monotheism, with the eradication of female deities and female symbolic powers bolstered patriarchy, which then reached its utmost radiance. Women were stripped of everything; Man was made in God's image while Woman was just an imperfect by-product of man and God! Like the first woman, Eve, they were seen from now-on as being supposedly made to obey and serve Man. Worse, since they were the descendants of the first 'sinner', they were supposed to be inhabited by sin, and in consequence couldn't be trusted or given any responsibility! They were excluded from the public sphere definitively, deprived of the few basic freedom and privileges they should normally enjoy. They were denied their humanity!

*

This story, (his)story, is not only unfair and sad, but also ignominiously perverse since it attests to an ongoing and continuous process of deliberately crushing women and transforming them into pets. It's a dark tale, an abject reality which has been -and still is- imposed on human beings whose only crime is to be female! Seen from this perspective, Patriarchy is not just a mere unjust historic wrong; it's a crime, an ignominious and despicable crime which has condemned women and girls to a dark and subhuman existence, made up of suffering, frustration and humiliation. It's a crime, not a historical mistake, because it was purposely orchestrated!

Patriarchy, the domination of a woman by a man, is not innate! It's a social construction that was made and that can be broken! And considering its despicable and indecent nature, and its counterproductive effect in modern societies -excluding or weakening half of the population's potential-, there is no reason not to change the rules to stop this detestable archaism which harms the people and threatens our common future.

'STRONG' AND 'INDEPENDENT' WOMEN:

THE DREAM MUST COME TRUE

Though the history of women during the past millenniums has been a tragedy that we cannot undo, the world is now changing at a fast pace and requires new rules and the participation of every citizen of Earth. We need a new age of enlightenment. Patriarchy as we know it is not sustainable -in the short or medium term- and changing nothing would only prevent societies becoming more efficient so that they could- confront the challenges posed by the modern -or post-modern- era.

Patriarchy feeds marginalization and inefficiency; it's a burden that we cannot afford anymore. It is making societies dysfunctional and can only jeopardize our common future. Fortunately, it is not based on any natural rule and, consequently, it is not intrinsically immutable nor irrevocable. Therefore, the necessity to evolve should call for a dramatic change to end patriarchy.

*

It is a sad statement to make but, today, women's empowerment is not merely a question of rights and ethics; it's an essential issue that will determine the levels of resilience of our communities, and of the world community as a whole. It is certainly not optional! Let us be clear: climate change, biodiversity losses, growing energy demand, demographic changes, economic unbalances, new technologies and their impact, risks of pandemics, international instability… are all factors of risk which require greater adaptability and higher efficiency. Hence, the urgent need to develop everyone's talents and skills, irrespective of their gender.

Social stereotypes, traditions, and religions commonly state that the gender division of labor is a natural consequence of some sort of genetic determinism. Complementarianism -a postulate put forward by Christianity, Judaism, and Islam- argue that men and women have different but complementary roles and responsibilities in marriage, family life, and religious leadership, thus justifying the alleged inability of women to perform the same tasks than men. But the reality today is quite different! In spite of the physiological and emotional dissimilarities which obviously distinguish women from men, both genders share equal intellectual potential and have the capacity to work in every field -if, of course, they are given a chance. According to an analysis published by the World Economic Forum in 2022, women are more productive than men: actually, they are assigned 10 percent more work than men these days (*"Women are more productive than men, according to new research", WEF*). It is the unequal access to education and economic and social opportunities that feeds the gender division of labor.

Men and women, boys and girls, males and females are sexually different, indeed; they have distinct physiology and psyche. But the recognition of the difference between two principles or genders doesn't necessarily imply a relationship of opposition or hierarchy. Genetic comparative studies of the XX and XY genes do not show any kind of 'inferiority' of the female principle… quite the contrary! There is no precept in Nature instating any domination of one sex over the other. Women and men are the two constituting elements of Mankind; they are interdependent and made to be so. Consequently, their relationship can only be successful and optimised if there is harmony between the two genders. But there is no real harmony if one suffers oppression because of the domination imposed by the other. Hence, the dysfunctional nature of patriarchy! Differences do not presuppose inequality.

But, if we agree that the two sexes are both equal and different, what does this mean in practice? What is it to be a 'free' or a 'strong' woman, equal to men in society? Since this very idea has no historical foundation and remains largely contradictory to traditions, the dominant image generally tends to depict a woman with a manly personality... some sort of masculinized -or de-feminized- woman. It is as if the feminine nature was incompatible with the notions of independence, authority, responsibility and power. This is wrong! Such a perspective only contributes to legitimized and strengthened patriarchy. A 'strong woman' doesn't have to be a muscular or masculine person; she doesn't have to think and behave like a man. Quite the contrary. A 'strong' woman is someone who is loving, who is caring, and who operates responsibly, with courage, who is independent and hopefully passionate. She's a liberated woman, entirely feminine; she acknowledges her feminine side and complies with her femininity...

The 'free' and 'strong' woman is not misandrist. She doesn't hate men. She is not dreaming of a world without men and doesn't want to harm them. Since Nature made the two sexes interdependent, being independent doesn't mean that we do not need someone; and this is true for both sexes. However, independence presupposes that we are determined to preserve our dignity! It means that we do not seek to take revenge and dominate men, but also that we refuse to be treated like a mere object: this is the true meaning of gender equality!

BIBLIOGRAPHY

Kacey Kells, "Kellcey", Olympia Publishers, London, 2017

Sarah B. Pommery, « Goddesses, Whores, Wives, and Slaves: Women in Classical Antiquity", Schoken Books, New York, 1995

Hilda Geissler, "The role of the goddesses and the feminine in ancient Egyptian religion". MPhil Thesis, University of Queensland
https://espace.library.uq.edu.au/view/UQ:312610

Yu Dong, Chelsea Morgan…: "Shifting diets and the rise of male-biased inequality on the Central Plains of China during Eastern Zhou"
https://www.researchgate.net/publication/312510719_Shifting_diets_and_the_rise_of_male-biased_inequality_on_the_Central_Plains_of_China_during_Eastern_Zhou

Mary Beard, "SPQR: a history of ancient Rome", Profile Books, London, 2016

Sheila Rowbotham, "Hidden from History, 300 Years of Women's Oppression and the Fight Against it", Pluto Press, London, 1992

Mary Wollstonecraft, "A Vindication of the Rights of Women", Penguin, London, 2004

Jean- I Jacques Rousseau, "Emile", Basic Books, New York, 1978

Sarah Zielinski, "Hypatia, Ancient Alexandria's Great Female Scholar", Smithsonian Magazine, March 2010 https://www.smithsonianmag.com/history/hypatia-ancient-alexandrias-great-female-scholar-10942888/

Pamela Jakiela & Susannah Hares, «Mind the Gap: 5 Facts About The Gender Gap in Education", Center for Global Development, Wahsindton, June 2017 https://www.cgdev.org/blog/mind-gap-5-facts-about-gender-gap-education

Rebecca Koehn, "Why Is There Still a Gender Gap in Tech?", Techopedia, Edmonto, Alberta, March 2022, https://www.techopedia.com/why-is-there-still-a-gender-gap-in-tech/2/34503

"Adult and Youth Literacy: Global trends in Gender Parity", UNESCO Institute for Statistics, September 2010 http://uis.unesco.org/sites/default/files/documents/fs3-adult-and-youth-literacy-global-trends-in-gender-parity-2010-en.pdf

Éloïse Trouche, "La place des femmes dans la recherche scientifique", Echo-Sciences Grenoble, avril 2020 https://www.echosciences-grenoble.fr/articles/la-place-des-femmes-dans-la-recherche-scientifique

Dale Debakcsy, "Theano of Croton And The Pythagorean Women Of Ancient Greece", Women you should know, February 2019 https://womenyoushouldknow.net/theano-of-croton-pythagorean/#google_vignette

"Gender Diversity", Informatics Europe, Zurich https://www.informatics-europe.org/activities/women-in-icst-research-and-education.html

Matthew Cobb, "Sexism in science: did Watson and Crick really steal Rosalind Franklin's data?", The Guardian, London, June 2015 https://www.theguardian.com/science/2015/jun/23/sexism-in-science-did-watson-and-crick-really-steal-rosalind-franklins-data

Jane Lee, "6 Women Scientists Who Were Snubbed Due to Sexism", National Geographic, May2013 https://www.nationalgeographic.com/culture/article/130519-women-scientists-overlooked-dna-history-science

Kaitlin Smith, "Nettie Maria Stevens (1861-1912)". Embryo Project Encyclopedia, Tmpe, Arizona, June 2010 https://embryo.asu.edu/pages/nettie-maria-stevens-1861-1912

Rebecca Ratcliffe, "Nobel scientist Tim Hunt: female scientists cause trouble for men in labs", the Guardian, London, June 2015 https://www.theguardian.com/uk-news/2015/jun/10/nobel-scientist-tim-hunt-female-scientists-cause-trouble-for-men-in-labs

"Women in Science", UNESCO Institute of Statistics, 2019, http://uis.unesco.org/sites/default/files/documents/fs55-women-in-science-2019-en.pdf

"Cyberbullying restricts young women's voices online", European Institute for Gender Equality, Vilnius, Lithuania, October 2018 https://eige.europa.eu/news/cyberbullying-restricts-young-womens-voices-online

"UN Women raises awareness of the shadow pandemic of violence against women during COVID-19", UN Women, May 27, 2020 https://twitter.com/UN_Women/status/1443479487027482624/photo/1

"The Luxury and the Lex Oppia, Rome and Art", RomeAndArt.eu, Rome, 30 October 2016, https://www.romeandart.eu/en/art-lex-oppia.html

"Cato the Elder is speaking, 195 BCE, on the repeal of the Lex Oppia; Livy 34.4-7", U. of Arizona http://www.u.arizona.edu/~afutrell/republic/web%20readings/livy34week10.html

I.M. Plant, "Women Writers of Ancient Greece and Rome", University. of Oklahoma Press, April 2004

Mary Beard, "Women and Power", Liveright Publishing Corporation, NY & London, 2017

Jared Yates Sexton, "There Will Be Blood: At a Donald Trump rally, supporters call for the death of Hillary Clinton", The new Republic, NY, July 6, 2016 https://newrepublic.com/article/134892/will-blood

"Witch Hunt Rhetoric At Trump Rallies Continues To Repel Women", Reverbpress.com, Washington, October 2016 https://reverbpress.com/politics/witch-hunt-rhetoric-hillary-clinton-will-stain-gop-forever/

Marie Berry, "Violence against women in politics", Political Violence at Glance, San Diego, November 2016 https://politicalviolenceataglance.org/2016/11/08/violence-against-women-in-politics/

Christine de Pisan, "The Book of the City of Ladies", Penguin Classics, 2000

"Seneca Falls Convention", History.com https://www.history.com/this-day-in-history/seneca-falls-convention-begins

Emma Goldman, "Anarchism and Other Essays", CreateSpace Independent Publishing Platform, 2016

Marge Berer, "Abortion Law and Policy Around the World", Health and Human Rights Journal, June 2017 https://www.ncbi.nlm.nih.gov/pmc/articles/PMC5473035/

"Unintended Pregnancy and Abortion Worldwide", Guttmacher Institute, Fact Sheet, July 2020 https://www.guttmacher.org/fact-sheet/induced-abortion-worldwide

"Rape Culture", Women's and Gender Center, Marshall University, https://www.marshall.edu/wcenter/sexual-assault/rape-culture/

Belinda Luscombe, "Kids Believe Gender Stereotypes by Age 10, Global Study Finds", Time Magazine, September 20, 2017 https://time.com/4948607/gender-stereotypes-roles/

Progress on the Sustainable Development Goals: The gender snapshot 2021", UN Women, https://www.unwomen.org/-media/headquarters/attachments/sections/library/publications/2021/progress-on-the-sustainable-development-goals-the-gender-snapshot-2021-en.pdf?la=en&vs=1057

"Learn the facts: Rural women and girls", UN Women, October 2021 https://www.unwomen.org/en/digital-library/multimedia/2018/2/infographic-rural-women

Lisa Warth, Malinka Koparanova, "Empowering Women for Sustainable Development", Discussion Papers Series 2012-1, United Nations Economic Commission for Europe, https://sustainabledevelopment.un.org/content/documents/549ece4.pdf

"Population, female % of total population", World Bank, https://data.worldbank.org/indicator/SP.POP.TOTL.FE.ZS

"India accounts for 45.8 million of world's missing females over last 50 years: UN report", The Print, June 2020, https://theprint.in/india/india-accounts-for-45-8-million-of-worlds-missing-females-over-last-50-years-un-report/451545/

"Why the majority of the world's poor are women?", OXFAM International, https://www.oxfam.org/en/why-majority-worlds-poor-are-women

"Women and hunger Facts", Hunger Notes, February 2016
www.worldhunger.org/women-and-hunger-facts/

"Progress on the Sustainable Development Goals: The gender snapshot
2021", UN Women, https://www.unwomen.org/-
media/headquarters/attachments/sections/library/publications/2021/pr
ogress-on-the-sustainable-development-goals-the-gender-snapshot-
2021-en.pdf?la=en&vs=1057

U.S. Bureau of Labor Statistics, April, 23, 2021,
https://www.bls.gov/opub/ted/2021/median-weekly-earnings-were-
900-for-women-1089-for-men-in-first-quarter-2021.htm

"Les inégalités femmes-hommes en 12 chiffres et 6 graphiques", Le
Monde, June 15, 2019, https://www.lemonde.fr/les-
decodeurs/article/2017/03/07/les-inegalites-hommes-femmes-en-12-
chiffres-et-6-graphiques_5090765_4355770.html

"Median weekly earnings for full-time employees in the United Kingdom
in 2020, by age and gender", Statista,
https://www.statista.com/statistics/800432/full-time-weekly-earnings-
uk-by-age-and-gender/

"How Will Divorce Affect Me Financially? ", YourDivorceQuestions.Org,
http://yourdivorcequestions.org/how-will-divorce-affect-me-financially/

Adam Smith, "The Wealth of Nations", University of Chicago Press, 1977

Alice H. Eagly, "The female psyche revisited: The importance of
communion: Understanding the contours of the sex/gender divide gives
insight into the female psyche", The General Psychologist, June 2017,
https://www.apadivisions.org/division-
1/publications/newsletters/general/2017/06/female-psyche

Simone de Beauvoir, "The Second Sex", Vintage Classics, Penguin,
London, 2015

Kate Millet, "Sexual Politics", University of Illinois Press, Chicago, 2000.

Richard A. Lippa, "Gender, Nature, and Nurture", Psychology Press, 2005

"Massive study reveals few differences between men and women's brains: Study by Rosalind Franklin University of Medicine and Science neuroscientists conduct meta-synthesis of three decades of research", EurekAlert, 25 march, 2021; American Association for the Advancement of Sciences AAS), https://www.eurekalert.org/news-releases/700086

Louann Brizendine, "The Female Brain", Transworld Publishers Ltd, 2008

Julie Scelfo, "Why Girls Will Be Girls", Newsweek, 30 July 2006, https://www.newsweek.com/why-girls-will-be-girls-112287

J. Ann Tickner, "Gender in International Relations: Feminist Perspectives on Achieving Global Security" Columbia University Press, 1992

Laura Sjoberg, "Introduction to Security Studies: Feminist Contributions", ResearchGate, April 2009, https://www.researchgate.net/publication/233316236_Introduction_to _Security_Studies_Feminist_Contributions

Esther Boserup, "Women's Role in Economic Development", Earthscan Publications, 2007

"Gender and development", OECD, https://www.oecd.org/development/gender-development/

"Sustainable Development". UNESCO. 3 August 2015, https://en.unesco.org/themes/education-sustainable-development/what-is-esd/sd

"Empowering Women for Sustainable Development", United Nations Economic Commission for Europe, 2012 https://unece.org/DAM/Gender/publications_and_papers/UNECE_Discu ssion_Paper_2012.1.pdf

"World Development Report 2012 : Gender Equality and Development",
World Bank Group, 2012,
https://openknowledge.worldbank.org/bitstream/handle/10986/4391/9
780821388105_overview.pdf?sequence=6&isAllowed=y

"World Development Report 2012 : Gender Equality and Development",
World Bank Group, Washington, 2012,
https://openknowledge.worldbank.org/bitstream/handle/10986/4391/9
780821388105_overview.pdf?sequence=6&isAllowed=y

Lourdes Beneria & al, "Gender, Development and Globalization:
Economics as if All People Mattered", Routledge, New York and London.
2016

"Gender in Chinese Philosophy", Internet Encyclopedia of Philosophy,
https://iep.utm.edu/gender-c/

Matt Ridley, "The Red Queen. Sex and Evolution in Human Nature",
Penguin Books, NY, London, 1993

"12 Neat Facts about the Y Chromosome", and "X Chromosome",
National Human Genome Research Institute,
https://www.genome.gov/about-genomics/fact-sheets/Y-Chromosome-
facts, https://www.genome.gov/genetics-glossary/X-Chromosome

Roseanne F. Zhao, "The Y chromosome: beyond gender determination",
National Human Genome Research Institute,
https://www.genome.gov/27557513/the-y-chromosome-beyond-
gender-determination

Natalie Angier, "Women, an Intimate Geography", Virago Press, London,
2014

J. Graves, J. Gecz, H. Hameister, "Evolution of the human X – a smart and
sexy chromosome that controls speciation and development", National

Center for Biotechnology Information, U.S. National Library of Medicine, 2002, https://pubmed.ncbi.nlm.nih.gov/12900556/

Charlotte England, "Children inherit their intelligence from their mother not their father, say scientists", the Independent, 23 December 2019, https://www.independent.co.uk/news/science/children-intelligence-iq-mother-inherit-inheritance-genetics-genes-a7345596.html

B Charlesworth, D Charlesworth, "The degeneration of Y chromosomes", National Center for Biotechnology Information, U.S. National Library of Medicine, Nov. 2000, https://pubmed.ncbi.nlm.nih.gov/11127901/

Liam Mannix, "X is greater than Y: Chromosomes may explain why women outlive men", The Sidney Morning Herald, March 2020, https://www.smh.com.au/national/x-is-greater-than-y-chromosomes-may-explain-why-women-outlive-men-20200303-p546cf.html

"AMH gene", Medline Plus, National Library of Medicine, https://medlineplus.gov/genetics/gene/amh/#conditions

"The Story Of X: Evolution Of A Sex Chromosome", Science Daily, April 2009,
https://www.sciencedaily.com/releases/2009/04/090416125209.htm

Virginia Woolf, "A room of One's Own", Penguin's Books, London, 2000

Elizabeth Anderson, "Feminist Epistemology: An Interpretation and a Defense", Hypatia, Vol. 10, No. 3, Summer 1995, http://www.mitspig.weebly.com/uploads/1/8/2/7/18272031/andersonfeid.pdf

Jeffery Haynes, Peter Hough…, "World Politics; International Relations and Globalization in the 21st Century", Sage, Los Angeles, 2017

"Women in Science", UNESCO Institute for Statistics, June 2019
http://uis.unesco.org/sites/default/files/documents/fs55-women-in-science-2019-en.pdf

"Advances in the Study of Behavior", Vol. 22, Academic Press, San Diego, 1993: Peter J.B. Slater, Manfred Milinski, "Male Aggression and Sexual Coercion of Females in Non-Human Primates and other Mammals" https://books.google.fr/books?id=rsheQy7E4loC&pg=PA32&lpg=PA32&dq=describing+the+influential+model+of+Wrangham&source=bl&ots=CjgNPuS9So&sig=ACfU3U0sFkLwfHmfhSFkp4qQTUMTIe8_8w&hl=en&sa=X&ved=2ahUKEwja6vWTta_3AhVhzoUKHWl9DHcQ6AF6BAgdEAM#v=onepage&q=describing%20the%20influential%20model%20of%20Wrangham&f=false

Paulette Delgado, "Women Outnumber Men at a Record High at US Universities", Institute for Future Education, Technologico de Monterey, Mexico, December 2021 https://observatory.tec.mx/edu-news/women-dominate-american-universities#:~:text=Women%20now%20outnumber%20men%20in,the%20United%20States%20are%20male.&text=Image%3A%20eggeeggjiew.,in%20higher%20education%20is%20rising

"Women Increasingly outnumber men at US colleges; but why?", Georgetown University, Washington, September 2021 https://feed.georgetown.edu/access-affordability/women-increasingly-outnumber-men-at-u-s-colleges-but-why/

"Women in EU Outnumber Men as Students & Graduates at Bachelor's & Master's Levels", Schengenvisainfonews, European Union, November 2021 https://www.schengenvisainfo.com/news/women-in-eu-outnumber-men-as-students-graduates-at-bachelors-masters-levels/#:~:text=According%20to%20the%20She%20Figures,differences%20between%20study%20fields%20remain.

"Women outnumber men in higher education but gender stereotyped subject choices persist", UNECE, September 2019 https://unece.org/statistics/news/women-outnumber-men-higher-education-gender-stereotyped-subject-choices-persist

"Facts and figures: Women's leadership and political participation", UNWomen, 2021, https://www.unwomen.org/en/what-we-do/leadership-and-political-participation/facts-and-figures

"The gender gap in employment: What's holding women back?", International Labor Organisation, February 2022 https://www.ilo.org/infostories/en-GB/Stories/Employment/barriers-women#intro

"Women now hold 32% of top leadership positions", Grant Thornton International Ltd, London, 2022 https://www.grantthornton.global/en/insights/women-in-business-2022/

"Vladimir Putin Just Signed Off on the Partial Decriminalization of Domestic Abuse in Russia", Time, London, February 2017 https://time.com/4663532/russia-putin-decriminalize-domestic-abuse/

"Women have paid the price for Trump's Regulatory Agenda", Center for American Progress, Washington, September 2020 https://www.independent.co.uk/news/world/americas/us-politics/trump-women-international-womens-day-abortion-policies-healthcare-a9380411.html

"Women and War: Women & Armed Conflicts and the issue of Sexual Violence", Institute for Security Studies, European Union & International Committee or the Red Cross, September 2014 file:///C:/Users/Bruno%20Munier/Downloads/icrc_report_women_and_war.pdf

Barbara Smuts, "Male Aggression against Women: An Evolutionary Perspective", University of Nebraska, Lincoln, 1992 https://www.unl.edu/rhames/courses/current/readings/smuts.pdf

Robert Wright, "he Moral Animal: Why We Are, the Way We Are: The New Science of Evolutionary Psychology", Vintage, Penguin, London, 1995

Gerda Lerner, "The Creation of Patriarchy", New York, Oxford University Press, 1986

Patricia Draper, "!Kung Women: Contrasts in Sexual Egalitarianism in Foraging and Sedentary Contexts", University of Nebraska, Lincoln, 1975 https://digitalcommons.unl.edu/cgi/viewcontent.cgi?referer=&httpsredi r=1&article=1044&context=anthropologyfacpub

"Women are more productive than men, according to new research", World Economic Forum, Geneva, New York, 2022 https://www.weforum.org/agenda/2018/10/women-are-more-productive-than-men-at-work-these-days